GO | STOP

SALVATION

GO | STOP

S A L V A T I O N

DR. RAY HAMPTON

Hunter Entertainment Network
4164 Austin Bluffs Parkway, Suite 214
Colorado Springs, Colorado 80918
www.hunter-ent-net.com

Each One Reach One
P.O. Box 591004
Fort Lauderdale, FL, United States 33359
www.rayhampton.com

This book and all other Hunter Entertainment Network™ Hunter Heart Publishing™, and Hunter Heart Kids™ books are available at Christian bookstores and distributors worldwide.

Chief Editor: Deborah G. Hunter
Book cover design: Chevy Cortez/www.ChevyCortez.com
ISBN: 978-0-9797679-1-3 (Seattle International Publishing)
Printed in the United States of America.

Table of Contents

Introduction

GO|STOP is an amazing evangelism and outreach tool that will empower and equip you to reach one person at a time. Many churches, ministries, and individuals have used GO|STOP to create a culture of soul winners within their church or ministry. GO|STOP is one of the most passionate, friendly, and effective methods of reaching out to the homeless, hopeless, helpless, rich, poor, and every nationality. The definition of GO|STOP means to *Go Out and Serve the Other Person.* In other words, STOP what you're doing and GO make DISCIPLES. If you are passionate about sharing the love of Jesus in your COMMUNITY, CITY, STATE, and the WORLD, then GO|STOP is for YOU!

"But you will receive power and ability when the Holy Spirit comes upon you; and you will be My witnesses [to tell people about Me] both in Jerusalem and in all Judea, and Samaria, and even to the ends of the earth." (Acts 1:8, AMP)

1

Foundation of Salvation

God has a rescue plan that is so simple that even the individual with no theological knowledge of biblical understanding can experience a transformed life with transforming power. Jesus Christ is not just the way to heaven or a way to heaven; He is the only way to heaven. The bridge between God and man is Jesus Christ. In order for Jesus to be a mediator for God, He had to become God and to represent man; He had to become a man Himself. The following scriptures explain the process:

1. Who was in the beginning?

"In the beginning was the _____, and the _____ was with God, and the _____ was God." (John 1:1, NKJV)

2. Who was with Christ in the beginning?
"In the beginning was the Word, and the Word was with _____, and the Word was _____." (John 1:1, NKJV)

3. What did the Word (Jesus) become?

"And the Word became _____ and dwelt among us, and we beheld His glory, the glory as of the only begotten of the Father, full of grace and truth." (John 1:14, NKJV)

4. The Word (Jesus) was full of what two things?

"And the Word became flesh and dwelt among us, and we beheld His glory, the glory as of the only begotten of the Father, full of _____ and _____." (John 1:14, NKJV)

5. How does a person get to God?

"_____ said to him, "I am the _____, the _____, and the _____. No one comes to the Father except through _____." (John 14:6, NKJV)

As Jesus, He serves as a mediator and an advocate. The mediator is the middle person mediating between two other people that are in disagreement with each other. Jesus is a mediator for believers and unbelievers between God and man. A man can mediate between two men, but he cannot mediate between a man and a horse without becoming, or having the nature of, a horse. So, Jesus could not mediate between God and man, unless He took on the nature of a man. Even though Jesus can be a mediator for the believer and unbeliever, He can only be an advocate for the believer. And unbeliever, which is a sinner, does not need an advocate; they need a Savior. What is the need for an advocate when the trial is over, the jury has given the verdict, the judge has pronounced sentencing, and the execution is set? What a condemned man needs is a pardon not an advocate, because they have already been found guilty and condemned. Take a look at the following scripture:

4

"For Your name's sake, O LORD, Pardon my iniquity, for it is great." (Psalms 25:11, NKJV)

"Keep up your reputation, GOD; Forgive my bad life; It's been a very bad life." (Psalm 25:11, MSG)

There is a difference between a sinner's sin; which is an unbeliever's sin and a believer's sin. One principal truth that is very clear is that God does not agree with anyone sinning. He actually hates the action of sin and He gets extremely upset when a believer sins. The difference is not in the sin, because there is no big sin or small sin; sin is sin. The difference is the way that God treats the sin. For example, read the following story. A father allowed his son to go outside to help a hired servant to clean the yard, but when the father looked out the window to see if they were cleaning the yard, to his amazement, they were both just sitting down on the ground being lazy not doing any work. He looked out the window again and noticed them sitting down doing nothing. The father sent the hired servant home, because he was lazy. Actually, his son was lazier than the hired servant, but he could not send his son home, because the son was already home. But, the father rebuked his son and took away his allowance. The son's punishment was worse than the hired servant. Why? Because the son and sonship is a shield from the punishment of sin. Sonship is not giving a believer a license to sin; sonship just gives the believer the blessed privilege of having an advocate in Jesus Christ. As long as you live on this earth, you will sin. It is better to commit an unintentional sin as a son, which is a believer, than an unbeliever that is not a son. As a born-again believer, you have not received the spirit of fear, but you have received the spirit of freedom from a sinner to Sonship to break every bondage. As adopted sons and daughters, you share the same rights and privileges as if you were naturally born into the family. This is the privilege for every Christian… as born-again believers; you have received the Spirit of Sonship and have the Holy Spirit in a measure. The other measure is given when the believer accepts truth and seeks God for the fullness.

SONSHIP THROUGH THE SPIRIT

1. If you live according to the flesh what will happen?
"For if you live according to the flesh you will _____; but if by the Spirit you put to death the deeds of the body, you will live." (Romans 8:13, NKJV)

2. If you live according to the spirit what will happen?
"For if you live according to the flesh you will die; but if by the Spirit you put to death the deeds of the body, you will _____." (Romans 8:13, NKJV)

3. If you are led by the Spirit, what does the scripture declare you to be?
"For as many as are led by the Spirit of God, these are _____ of _____." (Romans 8:14, NKJV)

4. As a believer in Christ, you did not receive the spirit of fear, but what spirit did you receive?
"For you did not receive the spirit of bondage again to fear, but you received the _____ of _____ by whom we cry out, "Abba, Father."" (Romans 8:15, NKJV)

5. According to scripture it says, "If you suffer with Christ," what will you also do?

"and if children, then heirs—heirs of God and joint heirs with Christ, if indeed we suffer with Him, that we may also be _____ _____." (Romans 8:17, NKJV)

Salvation, or to be born-again, is something that an individual person cannot accomplish on their own without the impartation process of the death of Jesus Christ on the cross and the impartation of the Holy Spirit and faith in God's Word. The reason why Jesus came to earth was to save the lost, because He knew that we could not save ourselves from the penalty a sin. Salvation is also the assurance of God's presence within every born-again believer. This is why Jesus is called Immanuel, which means God is with us, as was prophesied by the prophet Isaiah.

6. What is the virgin child name?

"Therefore the Lord Himself will give you a sign: Behold, the virgin shall conceive and bear a Son, and shall call His name _____." (Isaiah 7:14, NKJV)

Jesus was God in the flesh, which means that God is literally among you, with you, in you, and through you. Remember as stated earlier, Jesus is not a way to heaven; He is the only way to heaven. Jesus is the gate that will open up and lead you to eternal life, because there is only one road that leads to eternal life with God. Salvation is a work that is done in our life by the work of the Holy Spirit. No one can predict or understand the way the Holy Spirit works in our life. No one can control their own physical birth; neither can anyone control their spiritual birth, because it is a gift from God through the Spirit.

BORN OF THE HOLY SPIRIT

1. Who was Nicodemus a ruler of?
"There was a man of the Pharisees named Nicodemus, a ruler of the _____." (John 3:1, NKJV)

2. When did Nicodemus come to Jesus?
"This man came to Jesus by _____ and said to Him, "Rabbi, we know that You are a teacher come from God; for no one can do these signs that You do unless God is with him." (John 3:2, NKJV)

3. What did Jesus tell Nicodemus to do if he wanted to see the Kingdom of God?
"Jesus answered and said to him, "Most assuredly, I say to you, unless one is _____ _____, he cannot see the kingdom of God." (John 3:3, NKJV)

4. What two things did Jesus tell Nicodemus he had to be born of?
"Jesus answered, "Most assuredly, I say to you, unless one is born of _____ and the _____, he cannot enter the kingdom of God." (John 3:5, NKJV)

Every individual that has accepted Jesus has become born-again through God's unmerited grace, not because of your own effort, ability, intelligent choice, or act of any kind of special service. You are born-again simply because of God's unmerited grace. There is no action or work that you can do to a obtain salvation, but there are plenty of things that you can do to maintain your salvation. God's intention is that your salvation you have received will result in acts of service, such as to help

8

and serve other people with kindness and not please yourself. We are not saved for our own benefit, but only to serve Jesus Christ and to build the Kingdom of God.

YOU ARE SAVED BY GRACE THROUGH FAITH TO BUILD THE KINGDOM OF GOD

1. A person becomes saved by what and through what?
"For by _____ you have been saved through _____, and that not of yourselves; it is the gift of God," (Ephesians 2:8, NKJV)

2. What are the five ministerial gifts given to the body of Christ?
"And He Himself gave some to be _____, some ____, some _____, and some _____ and _____," (Ephesians 4:11, NKJV)

3. What are the five ministerial gifts given for?
"... for the _____ of the saints for the work of _____, for the _____ of the body of Christ," (Ephesians 4:12, NKJV)

THE PARABLE OF THE GREAT SUPPER

1. What was the first man's excuse for not coming to the supper?
"But they all with one accord began to make excuses. The first said to him, 'I have bought a _____ of _____, and I must go and see it. I ask you to have me excused.'" (Luke 14:18, NKJV)

2. What was the second man's excuse for not coming to the supper?
"And another said, 'I have bought _____ _____ of _____, and I am going to test them. I ask you to have me excused.'" (Luke 14:19, NKJV)

3.   What was the third man's excuse for not coming to the supper? "Still another said, 'I have _____ a _____, and therefore I cannot come.'" (Luke 14:20, NKJV)

4.   When everyone that was invited to the supper began to make excuses, what was the servant told to do?
"So that servant came and reported these things to his master. Then the master of the house, being angry, said to his servant, 'Go out quickly into the _____ and _____ of the _____, and bring in here the poor and the maimed and the lame and the blind." (Luke 14:21, NKJV)

5. When the servant told the master there still was more room, what was the servant told to do?
"Then the master said to the servant, 'Go out into the _____ and _____, and _____ them to come in, that my house may be filled." (Luke 14:23, NKJV)

6.   What were the three things the servant was told to do when inviting people to the supper? _____ _____ _____

"Then He said to him, "A certain man gave a great supper and _____ many," (Luke 14:16, NKJV)

"So that servant came and reported these things to his master. Then the master of the house, being angry, said to his servant, 'Go out quickly into the streets and lanes of the city, and _____ in here the poor and the maimed and the lame and the blind." (Luke 14:21, NKJV)

"Then the master said to the servant, 'Go out into the highways and hedges, and _____ them to come in, that my house may be filled." (Luke 14:23, NKJV)

This man who was sitting at the table with Jesus saw the manifest glory of God's Kingdom. But, one thing that was lacking in his life was how to get into heaven. In the preceding text of the banquet, many people turned down the invitation, because the timing was inconvenient. There are many people today that are doing the same thing; they are resisting, or delaying responding to, God's invitation of salvation. Even though their excuse might sound reasonable, such as work, family responsibilities, or financial needs, God's invitation to salvation is the most important decision that they will ever make in their life. Jesus reminded us in the text that the time will come when God will pull His invitation and offer it to another. Don't wait until it's too late to get into the banquet.

It was customary to send invitations to a party. The first invitation announced the event and the second invitation was to tell the guests that everything is now ready. The first invitation was the "save the date" and the second invitation was the actual announcement of what was to happen at the party. The guests of Jesus insulted Him by starting to make excuses when He had issued the second invitation. In the history of Israel, God's first invitation came from Moses and the prophets. The second invitation came from His son Jesus. The religious leaders accept-ed the first "save the date" invitation. They believed that God had called them to be His people, but they insulted God by refusing to accept His son just like the master sent his servant into the streets to invite the needy to his banquet. God has sent His son Jesus to tell you the party is ready!

HOW DO YOU BECOME A CHILD OF GOD?

"But to as many as did receive and welcome Him, He gave the authority (power, privilege, right) to become the children of God, that is, to those who believe in (adhere to, trust in, and rely on) His name–[Isaiah 56:5.] Who owe their birth neither to bloods nor to the will of the flesh [that of physical impulse] nor to the will of man [that of a natural father], but to God. [They are born of God!]" (John 1:12-13, AMPC)

1. How do you become a child of God?
"But as many as _____ _____, to them gave he power to become the sons of God, even to them that believe on his name:" (John 1:12, KJV)

The word "power" in this verse is not dunamis power like dynamite, physical power, but *exousia* power, which is delegated power or authority to become the sons or *Tekna* of God, which means children of God. You will not be able to receive Jesus if you don't believe there is a Jesus. To believe Jesus as a verb, it must come with a preposition, such as do you believe in Jesus, into Jesus, or upon Jesus. You can stand next to a chair and believe that it will hold you up, but it is actually not holding you up. Why? Because you are only using your head knowledge. If you believe into the chair by sitting down in the chair, you are now committing your entire weight to it and the chair is now holding you up. It is not good enough just to stand next to Jesus and say that He is holding you up. You have to commit your whole body to Him, so that He can hold you up.

"Commit your way to the Lord [roll and repose each care of your load on Him]; trust (lean on, rely on, and be confident) also in Him and He will bring it to pass." (Psalm 37:5, AMPC)

"Lean on, trust in, and be confident in the Lord with all your heart and mind and do not rely on your own insight or understanding." (Proverbs 3:5, AMPC)

Understanding cannot hold you up for a long period of time, but Jesus can hold you up for eternity. Now looking back at our text, John chapter one verse twelve, it starts out by saying, "As many as received him." That implies that the Gospel, which is the good news of Jesus, once it is believed, it only benefits the individual that receives it. Read the following scriptures and let it minister to YOU!

"Trust GOD from the bottom of your heart; don't try to figure out everything on your own. Listen for GOD's voice in everything you do, everywhere you go; he's the one who will keep you on track. Don't assume that you know it all. Run to GOD! Run from evil! Your body will glow with health, your very bones will vibrate with life! Honor GOD with everything you own; give him the first and the best. Your barns will burst, your wine vats will brim over. But don't, dear friend, resent GOD's discipline; don't sulk under his loving correction. It's the child he loves that GOD corrects; a father's delight is behind all this." (Proverbs 3:5-12, MSG)

DO YOU WANT TO HAVE AN EVERLASTING LIFE IN JESUS? YOU CAN HAVE IT TODAY; THIS IS WHY GOD SENT HIS SON JESUS INTO THE WORLD.

1. Because loves the world so much, what did he do?
"For God so loved the world that He _____ His only _____ _____ , that whoever believes in Him should not perish but have everlasting life." (John 3:16, NKJV)

2. How can you have everlasting life?
"For God so loved the world that He gave His only begotten Son, that whoever _____ in _____ should not _____ but have _____ life." (John 3:16, NKJV)

3. Why did God send his son into the world?
"For God did not send His Son into the world to condemn the world, but that the _____ through Him _____ be _____." (John 3:17, NKJV)

"This is how much God loved the world: He gave His Son, His one and only Son. And this is why: so that no one need be destroyed; by believing in Him, anyone can have a whole and lasting life. God didn't go to all the trouble of sending His Son merely to point an accusing finger, telling the world how bad it was. He came to help, to put the world right again. Anyone who trusts in Him is acquitted; anyone who refuses to trust Him has long since been under the death sentence without knowing it. And why? Because of that person's failure to believe in the one-of-a-kind Son of God when introduced to him." (John 3:16-18, MSG)

The preceding text says that "whoever believes in Him should not perish but have everlasting life." The Greek word *aionios* means to have unknown time, time out of mind or eternity. Eternal life itself is eternal; depending on who you are going to commit to, trust and dependency will decide your eternity. It's eternal because it is life. You can have it in

14

heaven or you can have it in hell. I would like to put it this way, either you're going to choose the smoking section or the non-smoking section, make a wise choice because either way, it's eternal. You're going to have to make a choice, according to the following scriptures it says:

"No one can serve two masters; for either he will hate the one and love the other, or he will be devoted to the one and despise the other. You cannot serve God and mammon [money, possessions, fame, status, or whatever is valued more than the Lord]." (Matthew 6:24, AMP)

"The thief comes only in order to steal and kill and destroy. I came that they may have and enjoy life, and have it in abundance [to the full, till it overflows]." (John 10:10, AMP)

4. What was Jesus' purpose for being born?
"The thief does not come except to steal, and to kill, and to destroy. I have come that they may have _____, and that they may have it more abundantly." (John 10:10, NKJV)

5. What type of life did Jesus say a person will have once they believe in Him?
"Most assuredly, I say to you, he who believes in Me has _____ _____."
(John 6:47, NKJV)

6. Where does Jesus cast our sins?
"He will again have compassion on us, And will subdue our iniquities. You will cast all our sins into the _____ of the _____." (Micah 7:19, NKJV)

15

I really like what the New Living Translation says about our sins that they are not just cast away into the sea, but the ocean. Seas are usually smaller and less deep than oceans. An ocean is a vast and a continuous frame of salty water that shelters almost seventy percent of the total earth's surface, while a sea is a large body of saline water that occupies a greater part of the world's surface, but is smaller than an ocean. So don't worry, there is enough room for all of your sins to fit.

"Once again you will have compassion on us. You will trample our sins under your feet and throw them into the depths of the ocean!" (Micah 7:19, NLT)

HOW CAN I BECOME A BORN-AGAIN BELIEVER IN CHRIST?

1. Is there anyone that is righteous?
"As it is written: "There is _____ righteous, no, _____ _____;" (Romans 3:10, NKJV)

2. Has anyone fallen short?
"... for _____ have _____ and _____ _____ of the glory of God," (Romans 3:23, NKJV)

3. How did God demonstrate His love toward us?
"But God demonstrates His own love toward us, in that while we were still _____, Christ _____ for _____." (Romans 5:8, NKJV)

4. Has everyone sinned?

"Therefore, just as through one man sin entered the world, and death through sin, and thus death spread to all men, because _____ _____." (Romans 5:12, NKJV)

5. What are the wages of sin and what is the gift of God?
"For the wages of sin is _____, but the gift of God is _____ _____ in Christ Jesus our Lord." (Romans 6:23, NKJV)

6. What does a person have to do to receive Jesus in their life?
"… that if you _____ with your _____ the Lord Jesus and _____ in your _____ that God has raised Him from the dead, you will be _____. For with the _____ one _____ unto righteousness, and with the _____ _____ is made unto _____." (Romans 10:9-10, NKJV)

7. What else does a person have to do to be saved?
"For "whoever _____ on the name of the LORD shall be _____." (Romans 10:13, NKJV)

8. After you heard the Gospel of salvation and received Jesus, what did the Holy Spirit do?
"In Him you also trusted, after you heard the word of truth, the gospel of your salvation; in whom also, having believed, you were _____ with the _____ _____ of _____, who is the _____ of our _____ until the redemption of the purchased possession, to the praise of His glory." (Ephesians 1:13-14, NKJV)

9. Once a person becomes a believer in Christ, what happens?

"Therefore, if anyone is in Christ, he is a ____ ____; old things have passed away; behold, all things have become new." (II Corinthians 5:17, NKJV)

WHAT DOES IT MEAN TO HAVE EVERLASTING LIFE?

1. Know ____ and His Son ____.
"… as You have given Him authority over all flesh, that He should give eternal life to as many as You have given Him. And this is eternal life, that they may know You, the only true ____, and ____ Christ whom You have sent." (John 17:2-3, NKJV)

2. How does a person come to Jesus?
"All that the Father gives Me will come to Me, and the one who comes to Me I will by no means cast out." (John 6:37, NKJV)

"No one can come to Me unless the ____ who sent Me draws him; and I will raise him up at the last day. It is written in the prophets, 'And they shall all be taught by God.' Therefore everyone who has heard and learned from the ____ comes to Me." (John 6:44-45, NKJV)

"And He said, "Therefore I have said to you that no one can come to Me unless it has been granted to him by My ____." (John 6:65, NKJV)

3. How does a believer in Christ listen and follow the instructions of Jesus?
"My sheep hear My ____, and I know them, and they ____ Me. And I give them eternal life, and they shall never perish; neither shall anyone snatch them out of My hand." (John 10:27-28, NKJV)

4. Does God condemn believers once they are in Christ?
"There is therefore now _____ _____ to those who are in Christ Jesus, who do not walk according to the flesh, but according to the Spirit." (Romans 8:1, NKJV)

5. Are believers in Christ free from the law of sin?
"For the law of the Spirit of life in Christ Jesus has made me _____ from the law of _____ and death. For what the law could not do in that it was weak through the _____ , God did by sending His own Son in the likeness of sinful _____ , on account of _____: He condemned _____ in the _____ , that the righteous requirement of the law might be fulfilled in us who do not walk according to the _____ but according to the _____ . For those who live according to the _____ set their minds on the things of the _____ , but those who live according to the _____ , the things of the _____ . For to be _____ minded is death, but to be _____ minded is life and peace. Because the _____ mind is enmity against God; for it is not subject to the law of God, nor indeed can be. So then, those who are in the _____ cannot please God. But you are not in the _____ but in the _____ , if indeed the _____ of _____ dwells in you. Now if anyone does not have the _____ of _____ he is not His. And if _____ is in you, the body is dead because of _____ but the _____ is _____ because of righteousness. But if the _____ of Him who raised Jesus from the dead dwells in you, He who raised _____ from the dead will also give life to your mortal bodies through His _____ who dwells in you. Therefore, brethren, we are debtors—not to the _____ , to live according to the flesh. For if you live according to the flesh you will die; but if by the Spirit you put to death the deeds of the body, you will live. For as many as are led by the Spirit of God, these are _____ of God." (Romans 8:2-14, NKJV)

19

When you become a new creation in Christ, you are no longer identified with the world's system.

6. Should a believer in Christ love everybody?

"Beloved, let us love one _____, for love is of God; and _____ who loves is born of God and knows God. He who does not love does not know God, for God is love." (I John 4:7-8, NKJV)

"Therefore if anyone is in Christ [that is, grafted in, joined to Him by faith in Him as Savior], he is a new creature [reborn and renewed by the Holy Spirit]; the old things [the previous moral and spiritual condition] have passed away. Behold, new things have come [because spiritual awakening brings a new life]." (II Corinthians 5:17, AMP)

Your new identity is now with Christ, because you have been baptized into the body of believers according to the Word of God.

"For by one [Holy] Spirit we were all baptized into one body, [spiritually transformed—united together] whether Jews or Greeks (Gentiles), slaves or free, and we were all made to drink of one [Holy] Spirit [since the same Holy Spirit fills each life]." (I Corinthians 12:13, AMP)

The proceeding scripture is talking about the baptism of the Holy Spirit and not the baptism in the Holy Spirit. It is the Holy Spirit that places you and I into the body of born-again believers, so that we can activate our God-given gifts to build up the body of Christ.

7. When I become a new believer in Christ, does my identity change?

"Therefore, if anyone is in Christ, he is a _____ _____; old things have passed away; behold, all things have become new." (II Corinthians 5:17, NKJV)

WHAT DOES IT MEAN TO HAVE EVERLASTING LIFE?

1. How are believers baptized into the body of Christ?

"For by _____ _____ we were all baptized into one body—whether Jews or Greeks, whether slaves or free—and have all been made to drink into _____ _____." (I Corinthians 12:13, NKJV)

"So, my dear children, don't let anyone divert you from the truth. It's the person who acts right who is right, just as we see it lived out in our righteous Messiah. Those who make a practice of sin are straight from the Devil, the pioneer in the practice of sin. The Son of God entered the scene to abolish the Devil's ways." (I John 3:7-8, MSG)

Your identification has been expired with the devil and has now been renewed with Christ. Verse eight starts out by saying, "He who sins is of the devil." I want you to recognize that the devil is the source for all sin and is the one responsible for bringing sin into the world. The reason why you and I have a sinful nature is because of the devil. Jesus told the religious leaders,

2. Is there any truth in the devil?

"You are of your father the devil, and the desires of your father you want to do. He was a murderer from the beginning, and does not stand in the _____, because there is _____ _____ in him. When he speaks a lie, he speaks from his own resources, for he is a _____ and the father of it." (John 8:44, NKJV)

21

Now depending whose nature you are carrying, that is whose nature you're going to imitate. The good news is in the next portion of the text, "For this purpose the son of God was manifested that he might destroy the works of the devil."

3. When John saw Jesus, what did he say?
"The next day John saw Jesus coming toward him, and said, _____ The Lamb of God who takes away the _____ of the world!" (John 1:29, NKJV)

Jesus died for the sin (singular) of the world and took away the penalty of sin (singular), and now your sins (plural) are behind you and never will be brought up again, as far as your salvation is concerned. It will only be people who will bring them up to you to remind you of how you used to be and what you used to do, but as far as Jesus is concerned, your sins are taken care of. IT IS FINISHED! I want you to really understand that it's the devil's business to employ people to do and accomplish his work, because the only way his work is going to get done is through people. But as believers in Jesus Christ, if we take care of our business, the devil will not be in our business. Whenever the enemy comes to remind you of your past, you remind him of his future. I am a born-again believer in Christ; you do not practice sin in me any longer. In first John chapter three verse four to nine it says:

"Whoever commits sin also commits lawlessness, and sin is lawlessness. And you know that He was manifested to take away our sins, and in Him there is no sin. Whoever abides in Him does not sin. Whoever sins has neither seen Him nor known Him. Little children, let no one deceive you. He who practices righteousness is righteous, just as He is righteous.

He who sins is of the devil, for the devil has sinned from the beginning. For this purpose the Son of God was manifested, that He might destroy the works of the devil. Whoever has been born of God does not sin, for His seed remains in him; and he cannot sin, because he has been born of God." (I John 3:4-9, NKJV)

4. What was Jesus manifested to do?
"And you know that He was manifested to take away our _____, and in Him there is no sin." (I John 3:5, NKJV)

5. Was there any sin in Jesus?
"And you know that He was manifested to take away our sins, and in _____ there is _____ ____." (I John 3:5, NKJV)

6. When you in abide in Jesus, will you practice sin?
"Whoever abides in Him _____ _____ sin. Whoever sins has neither seen Him nor known Him." (I John 3:6, NKJV)

7. When you practice righteousness, what are you?
"Little children, let no one deceive you. He who practices righteousness is _____, just as He is _____." (I John 3:7, NKJV)

When you become born-again, you will not want to practice sin anymore. The text says when you are born of God, you will not commit sin. The Greek word for commit is *poieo* (poy-eh'-o), which means to exercise, continue, or practice. The Greek word for sin is *hamartia* (ham-ar-tee-ah), which is sin. As a born-again believer, you have received a new identity when you became born-again. Your new identity will not and cannot practice sin. The reason why the prodigal son could

23

not stay in the pig pen is because he was not a pig. You might be wondering what does it means to be a prodigal person. It is a person that
leaves home and behaves recklessly, but later makes a repentant return
back home.

“When he finally came to his senses, he said to himself, ‘At home even
the hired servants have food enough to spare, and here I am dying of
hunger! I will go home to my father and say, “Father, I have sinned
against both heaven and you,” (Luke 15:17-18, NLT)

As I already stated, the prodigal son could not stay in the pig pen.
Why? Because he was not a pig, which is the same reason why you can't
stay in the pig pen. Why? Because we have been born-again and we are
children of God. As a born-again believer, you should never feel com-
fortable living in sin.

“My dear children, I am writing this to you so that you will not sin. But
if anyone does sin, we have an advocate who pleads our case before the
Father. He is Jesus Christ, the one who is truly righteous.” (I John 2:1,
NLT)

The word “advocate” is from the Greek word *parakletos*, which is
translated “comforter”. The Holy Spirit is your comforter here on earth
and Christ is your comforter in heaven. An advocate or *parakletos* is a
legal term that means “One who will come to your side to help in your
time of need.”

“Then I heard a loud voice saying in heaven, “Now salvation, and
strength, and the kingdom of our God, and the power of His Christ have

come, for the accuser of our brethren, who accused them before our God day and night, has been cast down. And they overcame him by the blood of the Lamb and by the word of their testimony, and they did not love their lives to the death." (Revelation 12:10-11, NKJV)

When you sin as a believer, it breaks fellowship with God. It's the devil that wants you to continue sinning as an exercise and practice sin, so he can accuse the born-again believer before God. The Holy Spirit is stronger and bigger than the accuser, who is the devil.

"This is the message [of God's promised revelation] which we have heard from Him and now announce to you, that God is Light [He is holy, His message is truthful, He is perfect in righteousness], and in Him there is no darkness at all [no sin, no wickedness, no imperfection]. If we say that we have fellowship with Him and yet walk in the darkness [of sin], we lie and do not practice the truth; but if we [really] walk in the Light [that is, live each and every day in conformity with the precepts of God], as He Himself is in the Light, we have [true, unbroken] fellowship with one another [He with us, and we with Him], and the blood of Jesus His Son cleanses us from all sin [by erasing the stain of sin, keeping us cleansed from sin in all its forms and manifestations]. If we say we have no sin [refusing to admit that we are sinners], we delude ourselves and the truth is not in us. [His word does not live in our hearts.] If we [freely] admit that we have sinned and confess our sins, He is faithful and just [true to His own nature and promises], and will forgive our sins and cleanse us continually from all unrighteousness [our wrongdoing, everything not in conformity with His will and purpose]. If we say that we have not sinned [refusing to admit acts of sin], we make Him [out to be] a liar [by contradicting Him] and His word is not in us." (I John 1:5-10, AMP)

8.   When you know to do what's right and refuse to do it, what does the Word of God call it?
"Therefore, to him who knows to do _____ and does not do it, to him it is _____." (James 4:17, NKJV)

"For it is by grace [God's remarkable compassion and favor drawing you to Christ] that you have been saved [actually delivered from judgment and given eternal life] through faith. And this [salvation] is not of yourselves [not through your own effort], but it is the [undeserved, gracious] gift of God; not as a result of [your] works [nor your attempts to keep the Law], so that no one will [be able to] boast or take credit in any way [for his salvation]." (Ephesians 2:8-9, AMP)

A lack of faith is what causes you to lose your salvation, not sin. Sin will cause you to harden your heart, which in return will cause you to lose your faith.

The Greek word for salvation is *soteriology*, which comes from the words *soteria* and *logos*. The word *soteria* means salvation and the word logos means word or doctrine. In the study of anthropology, which is the doctrine of man and hamartiology, which is the doctrine of sin, we can see the failure of sin of man. Because of sin, there had to be a plan of salvation to bridge the gap between man and God, which is the sinfulness of man on one side of the bridge and the holiness of God on the other side of the bridge. Because of the greatness of God's ability to be omnipresent, which means that God is everywhere, His omnipotence

26

shows that He has all power and omniscience, which means that God sees everything. God already knew the fall of man before man failed.

"… just as He chose us in Him before the foundation of the world, that we should be holy and without blame before Him in love," (Ephesians 1:4, NKJV)

God had a plan, which was to send His Son Jesus to provide a way of escape for every non-believer from condemnation of sin.

9.   When you are in Christ, is there any condemnation?
"There is therefore now no condemnation to those who are in Christ Jesus, who do not walk according to the flesh, but according to the Spirit." (Romans 8:1, NKJV)

10. As a believer in Jesus Christ, what two things are you free from?
"For the law of the Spirit of life in Christ Jesus has made me free from the law of sin and death." (Romans 8:2, NKJV)

11. As believers in Jesus Christ, we do not walking according to the flesh, but what do walk according to?
"… that the righteous requirement of the law might be fulfilled in us who do not walk according to the flesh but according to the Spirit." (Romans 8:4, NKJV)

12. As a believer, when you walk according to the flesh, what happens to your mind?

13. As a believer when you are walking according to the Spirit, what happens?

"For those who live according to the flesh _____ their minds on the things of the _____, but those who live according to the Spirit, the _____ of the Spirit." (Romans 8:5, NKJV)

14. What is the result of being carnally-minded?

15. What is the result of being spiritually-minded?

16. When you are faced with temptation, what will God not allow you to be?

"No temptation has _____ you except such as is common to man; but God is faithful, who will not allow you to be tempted _____ what you are _____, but with the temptation will also make the way of _____, that you may be able to bear it." (I Corinthians 10:13, NKJV)

17. What will God do with the temptation?

"No temptation has overtaken you except such as is common to man; but God is faithful, who will not allow you to be tempted beyond what you are able, but with the temptation will also make the way of _____, that you may be able to bear it." (I Corinthians 10:13, NKJV)

"No test or temptation that comes your way is beyond the course of what others have had to face. All you need to remember is that God will never let you down; he'll never let you be pushed past your limit; he'll always be there to help you come through it." (I Corinthians 10:13, MSG)

Romans chapter eight verses one through eleven will let every born-again believer know that you, as a child of God, have assurance of the eternal keeping power of God in all temptations, providing that you are obedient according to the previous verses. God will not keep you from falling if you are going to keep practicing sin and continue to be persistent in refusing to meet the conditions of Scripture. For you not to fall consistently and stand firm on the foundation of the Word, depends upon your faith and prayer life. The strongest born-again believer can only stand as long as they depend on and obey the Word of God.

"Trust in the LORD with all your heart, And lean not on your own understanding; In all your ways acknowledge Him, And He shall direct your paths." (Proverbs 3:5-6, NKJV)

"Trust GOD from the bottom of your heart; don't try to figure out everything on your own. Listen for GOD's voice in everything you do, everywhere you go; he's the one who will keep you on track. Don't assume that you know it all. Run to GOD! Run from evil! Your body will glow with health, your very bones will vibrate with life! Honor GOD with everything you own; give him the first and the best. Your barns will burst, your wine vats will brim over. But don't, dear friend, resent GOD's discipline; don't sulk under his loving correction. It's the child he loves that GOD corrects; a father's delight is behind all this." (Proverbs 3:5-12, MSG)

Whenever you reject the conditions of living right, you will not and cannot escape eternal death and punishment.

"… lest Satan should take advantage of us; for we are not ignorant of his devices." (II Corinthians 2:11, NKJV)

The Greek word *noema* for "devices" means that you, as a born-again believer, should not be ignorant of the devil's thoughts, purposes, or designs.

"Be sober, be vigilant; because your adversary the devil walks about like a roaring lion, seeking whom he may devour." (I Peter 5:8, NKJV)

You should never be ignorant of the devil's thoughts. Why? Because the Word of God says, so read the following verses.

"Now I, Paul, myself am pleading with you by the meekness and gentleness of Christ— who in presence am lowly among you, but being absent am bold toward you. But I beg you that when I am present I may not be bold with that confidence by which I intend to be bold against some, who think of us as if we walked according to the flesh. For though we walk in the flesh, we do not war according to the flesh. For the weapons of our warfare are not carnal but mighty in God for pulling down strongholds, casting down arguments and every high thing that exalts itself against the knowledge of God, bringing every thought into captivity to the obedience of Christ, and being ready to punish all disobedience when your obedience is fulfilled." (II Corinthians 10:1-6, NKJV)

18. What can you do through Christ?
"I can do all things through Christ who strengthens me." (Philippians 4:13, NKJV)

This scripture is confirming that with Christ, super power on your natural power, you will always be able to do the supernatural. So, when it comes to casting down imaginations, you can demolish all theories, reasoning, any high system of ethics, religion, mythology, metaphysics, sublime doctrines, or philosophy that tries to go against the knowledge of God, which is the Word of God. As a believer in Christ, you can bring every thought into captivity and make that thought obey the Word of God. The thought that I am speaking of is any thinking which is contrary to the Word of God that would cause you to be unrighteous.

"And now, dear brothers and sisters, one final thing. Fix your thoughts on what is true, and honorable, and right, and pure, and lovely, and admirable. Think about things that are excellent and worthy of praise." (Philippians 4:8, NLT)

"The thoughts of the wicked are an abomination to the LORD, But the words of the pure are pleasant." (Proverbs 15:26, NKJV)

WHAT DOES IT MEAN TO TRIUMPH IN CHRIST?

"Now thanks be to God who always leads us in triumph in Christ, and through us diffuses the fragrance of His knowledge in every place." (II Corinthians 2:14, NKJV)

To triumph in Christ means to have complete control over satanic powers in your life.

"In Him you were also circumcised with the circumcision made without hands, by putting off the body of the sins of the flesh, by the circumci-

31

sion of Christ, buried with Him in baptism, in which you also were raised with Him through faith in the working of God, who raised Him from the dead. And you, being dead in your trespasses and the uncircumcision of your flesh, He has made alive together with Him, having forgiven you all trespasses, having wiped out the handwriting of requirements that was against us, which was contrary to us. And He has taken it out of the way, having nailed it to the cross. Having disarmed principalities and powers, He made a public spectacle of them, triumphing over them in it. So let no one judge you in food or in drink, or regarding a festival or a new moon or Sabbaths, which are a shadow of things to come, but the substance is of Christ." (Colossians 2:11-17, NKJV)

"Tell me, you who desire to be under the law, do you not hear the law?" (Galatians 4:21, NKJV)

Did you know that all laws were abolished in Christ?

1. After an unbeliever repents, what immediately happens afterwards?
"Repent therefore and be _____, that your sins may be blotted out, so that times of refreshing may come from the presence of the Lord," (Acts 3:19, NKJV)

2. What happens to your sins once you have repented and have been converted?
"Repent therefore and be converted, that your sins may be _____ _____, so that times of refreshing may come from the presence of the Lord," (Acts 3:19, NKJV)

The Greek word for blotted out is *exaleipho*, which means to smear out or be wiped away. There are two conditions necessary for forgiveness:

Every person has to repent; the Greek word *metanoia* means to change the mind and attitude toward sin.

"IN THOSE days there appeared John the Baptist, preaching in the Wilderness (Desert) of Judea And saying, Repent (think differently; change your mind, regretting your sins and changing your conduct), for the kingdom of heaven is at hand." (Matthew 3:1-2, AMPC)

"From that time Jesus began to preach, crying out, Repent (change your mind for the better, heartily amend your ways, with abhorrence of your past sins), for the kingdom of heaven is at hand." (Matthew 4:17, AMPC)

The word "repentance" is one of the main key words in the Bible. Repentance is located throughout the Bible about one hundred and ten times, starting in Genesis the sixth chapter verse six to Revelation the sixteenth chapter verse eleven.

GENESIS: "And it repented the Lord that he had made man on the earth, and it grieved him at his heart." (Genesis 6:6, KJV)

REVELATION: "And blasphemed the God of heaven because of their pains and their sores, and repented not of their deeds." (Revelation 16:11, KJV)

3. What are the eight equal words for repentance? _____,
_____,_____,_____,_____,_____and
_____.

4. To Be _____.
"And the LORD was _____ that He had made man on the earth, and He was grieved in His heart." (Genesis 6:6, NKJV)

5. To Turn _____.
"Therefore say to the house of Israel, 'Thus says the Lord GOD: "Repent, turn _____ from your idols, and turn your faces _____ from all your abominations." (Ezekiel 14:6, NKJV)

6. To Regret _____.
"I will ransom them from the power of the grave; I will redeem them from death. O Death, I will be your plagues! O Grave, I will be your destruction! Pity is hidden from My eyes." (Hosea 13:14, NKJV)

7. _____.
"How can I give you up, O Ephraim? How can I hand you over, O Israel? How can I make you like Admah? How can I treat you like Zeboiim? My heart recoils within me; my _____ grows warm and tender." (Hosea 11:8, ESV)

8. To regret the consequences of sin, not the cause.
"Then when Judas, his betrayer, saw that Jesus was condemned, he changed his mind and brought back the thirty pieces of silver to the chief priests and the elders," (Matthew 27:3, ESV)

9. _____.

"For God's gifts and His call are _____. [He never withdraws them when once they are given, and He does not change His mind about those to whom He gives His grace or to whom He sends His call.]" (Romans 11:29, AMPC)

10. A change of mind and attitude toward sin and its cause, but not the consequences.

"So produce fruit that is consistent with repentance [demonstrating new behavior that proves a change of heart, and a conscious decision to turn away from sin];" (Matthew 3:8, AMP)

11. To change the mind and attitude toward sin.

"Just at that time some people came who told Jesus about the Galileans whose blood Pilate [the governor] had mixed with their sacrifices. Jesus replied to them, "Do you think that these Galileans were worse sinners than all other Galileans because they have suffered in this way? I tell you, no; but unless you repent [change your old way of thinking, turn from your sinful ways and live changed lives], you will all likewise perish. Or do you assume that those eighteen on whom the tower in Siloam fell and killed were worse sinners than all the others who live in Jerusalem? I tell you, no; but unless you repent [change your old way of thinking, turn from your sinful ways and live changed lives], you will all likewise perish." (Luke 13:1-5, AMP)

In the preceding text Jesus is letting you know that there is no difference between a big sin and small sin. It's only the enemy the devil that would have you to categorize sin. A lying spirit is just as bad as a backbiting spirit, adultery spirit is just as bad as a fornication spirit,

GO|STOP SALVATION

idolatry sprit is just as bad as a witchcraft spirit, a hatred sprit is just as bad as a jealous spirit, a envy sprit is just as bad as a murder spirit and a drunkenness sprit is just as bad as an overeating sprit. What Jesus wants you to understand is that there are no big sins or small sins, sin is sin. The following scripture will show that everyone is equally sinners and condemned before God.

"For everyone has sinned; we all fall short of God's glorious standard." (Romans 3:23, NLT)

The second condition is to be converted, which means to change your conduct and turn around and make a change in direction and begin a new walk toward God and with God.

12. What is the law of the Lord and what does it do?
"The law of the LORD is ____, _____ the soul; The testimony of the LORD is sure, making wise the simple;" (Psalms 19:7, NKJV)

13. Who are sinners converted to?
"Then I will teach transgressors Your ways, And sinners shall be converted to You." (Psalms 51:13, NKJV)

The Word God says to be converted: meaning to turn back, retreat, recover, restore, or to bring back.

14. Why does an unbeliever need to be converted?
"and said, "Assuredly, I say to you, unless you are converted and become as little children, you will by no means enter the kingdom of

heaven. Therefore whoever humbles himself as this little child is the greatest in the kingdom of heaven." (Matthew 18:3-4, NKJV)

15. If a sinner starts to walk away from the truth, what should you do as a believer?
"Brethren, if anyone among you wanders from the truth, and someone _____ him back, let him know that he who _____ a sinner from the error of his way will save a soul from death and cover a multitude of sins." (James 5:19-20, NKJV)

"My dear friends, if you know people who have wandered off from God's truth, don't write them off. Go after them. Get them back and you will have rescued precious lives from destruction and prevented an epidemic of wandering away from God." (James 5:19-20, MSG)

"And the Lord said, "Simon, Simon! Indeed, Satan has asked for you, that he may sift you as wheat. But I have prayed for you, that your faith should not fail; and when you have returned to Me, strengthen your brethren." (Luke 22:31-32, NKJV)

"Simon, stay on your toes. Satan has tried his best to separate all of you from me, like chaff from wheat. Simon, I've prayed for you in particular that you not give in or give out. When you have come through the time of testing, turn to your companions and give them a fresh start." (Luke 22:31-32, MSG)

The preceding scripture is not saying that Peter is not saved or converted; Peter had served God for over three years. This text is referring to the fact that Peter was headed for a fall, but not that he had fallen and that he would come back to God and be reconverted, which made him become stronger than before. A new rechargeable battery that has lost its energy because of use is still a battery, but when it is plugged back into the power source, it will become recharged and stronger. It's the same with you as a believer that has been converted. Whenever you begin to start losing your power, all you have to do is reconnect yourself back up to the power source, which is Jesus and at that very moment, you have instantly started the process of being recharged and becoming stronger than before. This is why whenever you go through trials in your life; your testimonies get stronger and stronger. Why? Because your miseries are now your ministries, your tests are now your testimonies, the pity party is now your praise party and many prayers have produced much power.

"And they overcame him by the blood of the Lamb and by the word of their testimony, and they did not love their lives to the death." (Revelation 12:11, NKJV)

WHEN AN UNBELIEVER IS CONVERTED TO A BELIEVER, IT IS ALWAYS GOING TO RESULT IN THE FOLLOWING:

1. A moral and spiritual change.
"There was a man of the Pharisees named Nicodemus, a ruler of the Jews. This man came to Jesus by night and said to Him, "Rabbi, we know that You are a teacher come from God; for no one can do these signs that You do unless God is with him." Jesus answered and said to him, "Most assuredly, I say to you, unless one is born again, he cannot see the kingdom of God." Nicodemus said to Him, "How can a man be born when he is old? Can he enter a second time into his mother's womb

and be born?" Jesus answered, "Most assuredly, I say to you, unless one is born of water and the Spirit, he cannot enter the kingdom of God. That which is born of the flesh is flesh, and that which is born of the Spirit is spirit. Do not marvel that I said to you, 'You must be born again.' The wind blows where it wishes, and you hear the sound of it, but cannot tell where it comes from and where it goes. So is everyone who is born of the Spirit." (John 3:1-8, NKJV)

2. A changed heart.

"Therefore if anyone is in Christ [that is, grafted in, joined to Him by faith in Him as Savior], he is a new creature [reborn and renewed by the Holy Spirit]; the old things [the previous moral and spiritual condition] have passed away. Behold, new things have come [because spiritual awakening brings a new life]. But all these things are from God, who reconciled us to Himself through Christ [making us acceptable to Him] and gave us the ministry of reconciliation [so that by our example we might bring others to Him]," (II Corinthians 5:17-18, AMP)

3. God's Adoption.

"Just as [in His love] He chose us in Christ [actually selected us for Himself as His own] before the foundation of the world, so that we would be holy [that is, consecrated, set apart for Him, purpose-driven] and blameless in His sight. In love He predestined and lovingly planned for us to be adopted to Himself as [His own] children through Jesus Christ, in accordance with the kind intention and good pleasure of His will." (Ephesians 1:4-5, AMP)

"... so that He might redeem and liberate those who were under the Law, that we [who believe] might be adopted as sons [as God's children with all rights as fully grown members of a family]." (Galatians 4:5, AMP)

4. Favor with a new standing before God.

"Therefore, having been justified by faith, we have peace with God through our Lord Jesus Christ, through whom also we have access by faith into this grace in which we stand, and rejoice in hope of the glory of God." (Romans 5:1-2, NKJV)

"It wasn't so long ago that you were mired in that old stagnant life of sin. You let the world, which doesn't know the first thing about living, tell you how to live. You filled your lungs with polluted unbelief, and then exhaled disobedience. We all did it, all of us doing what we felt like doing, when we felt like doing it, all of us in the same boat. It's a wonder God didn't lose his temper and do away with the whole lot of us. Instead, immense in mercy and with an incredible love, he embraced us. He took our sin-dead lives and made us alive in Christ. He did all this on his own, with no help from us! Then he picked us up and set us down in highest heaven in company with Jesus, our Messiah.

Now God has us where he wants us, with all the time in this world and the next to shower grace and kindness upon us in Christ Jesus. Saving is all his idea, and all his work. All we do is trust him enough to let him do it. It's God's gift from start to finish! We don't play the major role. If we did, we'd probably go around bragging that we'd done the whole thing! No, we neither make nor save ourselves. God does both the making and saving. He creates each of us by Christ Jesus to join him in the work he does, the good work he has gotten ready for us to do, work we had better be doing." (Ephesians 2:1-10, MSG)

5. As a believer in Jesus, when you practice righteousness, who does the Word of God say that you are?

"Little children, let no one deceive you. He who practices righteousness is _____, just as He is righteous. He who sins is of the devil, for the devil has sinned from the beginning. For this purpose the Son of God was manifested, that He might destroy the works of the devil. Whoever has been born of God does not sin, for His seed remains in him; and he cannot sin, because he has been born of God. In this the children of God and the children of the devil are manifest: Whoever does not practice righteousness is not of God, nor is he who does not love his brother." (I John 3:7-10, NKJV)

"So, my dear children, don't let anyone divert you from the truth. It's the person who acts right who is right, just as we see it lived out in our righteous Messiah. Those who make a practice of sin are straight from the Devil, the pioneer in the practice of sin. The Son of God entered the scene to abolish the Devil's ways.

People conceived and brought into life by God don't make a practice of sin. How could they? God's seed is deep within them, making them who they are. It's not in the nature of the God-begotten to practice and parade sin. Here's how you tell the difference between God's children and the Devil's children: The one who won't practice righteous ways isn't from God, nor is the one who won't love brother or sister. A simple test." (I John 3:7-10, MSG)

41

NOW THAT THE PERSON HAS BEEN CONVERTED, WHAT HAPPENS IF THEY COMMIT A SIN?

1. If any man sins, he has an advocate. What is an advocate for? To restore an individual back to Jesus Christ.

2. What does a believer in Christ have when they sin?
"My little children, these things I write to you, so that you may not sin. And if anyone sins, we have an _____ with the Father, Jesus Christ the righteous. And He Himself is the propitiation for our sins, and not for ours only but also for the whole world." (I John 2:1-2, NKJV)

3. When you confess your sins, what will Jesus do?
"If we confess our sins, He is faithful and just to _____ us our sins and to _____ us from all _____." (I John 1:9, NKJV)

"If we claim that we're free of sin, we're only fooling ourselves. A claim like that is errant nonsense. On the other hand, if we admit our sins— make a clean breast of them—he won't let us down; he'll be true to himself. He'll forgive our sins and purge us of all wrongdoing. If we claim that we've never sinned, we out-and-out contradict God—make a liar out of him. A claim like that only shows off our ignorance of God." (I John 1:8-10, MSG)

4. Paul taught that God is able to graft a person again.
"But you must not brag about being grafted in to replace the branches that were broken off. You are just a branch, not the root. "Well," you may say, "those branches were broken off to make room for me." Yes, but remember—those branches were broken off because they didn't

believe in Christ, and you are there because you do believe. So don't think highly of yourself, but fear what could happen. For if God did not spare the original branches, he won't spare you either. Notice how God is both kind and severe. He is severe toward those who disobeyed, but kind to you if you continue to trust in his kindness. But if you stop trusting, you also will be cut off. And if the people of Israel turn from their unbelief, they will be grafted in again, for God has the power to graft them back into the tree. You, by nature, were a branch cut from a wild olive tree. So if God was willing to do something contrary to nature by grafting you into his cultivated tree, he will be far more eager to graft the original branches back into the tree where they belong." (Romans 11:18-24, NLT)

5. James taught a reconversion after a believer sins.
"My brothers, if anyone among you wanders from the truth and someone brings him back," (James 5:19, ESV)

"My dear friends, if you know people who have wandered off from God's truth, don't write them off. Go after them. Get them back and you will have rescued precious lives from destruction and prevented an epidemic of wandering away from God." (James 5:19-20, MSG)

6. What did Paul say to do for a person that is practicing sin?
"BRETHREN, IF any person is overtaken in misconduct or sin of any sort, you who are spiritual [who are responsive to and controlled by the Spirit] should set him right and _____ and _____ him, without any sense of superiority and with all gentleness, keeping an attentive eye on yourself, lest you should be tempted also." (Galatians 6:1, AMPC)

7. Jesus taught reconversion.

"~'But I have this [charge] against you, that you have left your first love [you have lost the depth of love that you first had for Me]. ~'So remember the heights from which you have fallen, and repent [change your inner self--your old way of thinking, your sinful behavior--seek God's will] and do the works you did at first [when you first knew Me]; otherwise, I will visit you and remove your lampstand (the church, its impact) from its place--unless you repent." (Revelation 2:4-5, AMP)

"But you walked away from your first love—why? What's going on with you, anyway? Do you have any idea how far you've fallen? A Lucifer fall! "Turn back! Recover your dear early love. No time to waste, for I'm well on my way to removing your light from the golden circle." (Revelation 2:4-5, MSG)

8. David was reconverted after he committed sin.

"Have mercy upon me, O God, According to Your lovingkindness; According to the multitude of Your tender mercies, Blot out my transgressions. Wash me thoroughly from my iniquity, And cleanse me from my sin. For I acknowledge my transgressions, And my sin is always before me. Against You, You only, have I sinned, And done this evil in Your sight— That You may be found just when You speak, And blameless when You judge. Behold, I was brought forth in iniquity, And in sin my mother conceived me. Behold, You desire truth in the inward parts, And in the hidden part You will make me to know wisdom. Purge me with hyssop, and I shall be clean; Wash me, and I shall be whiter than snow. Make me hear joy and gladness, That the bones You have broken may rejoice. Hide Your face from my sins, And blot out all my iniquities. Create in me a clean heart, O God, And renew a steadfast spirit within me. Do not cast me away from Your presence, And do not take Your Holy Spirit from me. Restore to me the joy of Your salvation, And uphold me by Your generous Spirit. Then I will teach transgressors Your ways, And sinners shall be converted to You. Deliver me from the guilt of bloodshed, O God, The God of my salvation, And my tongue shall sing aloud of Your righteousness. O Lord, open my lips, And my mouth shall show forth Your praise." (Psalms 51:1-15, NKJV)

"Generous in love—God, give grace! Huge in mercy—wipe out my bad record. Scrub away my guilt, soak out my sins in your laundry. I know how bad I've been; my sins are staring me down. You're the One I've violated, and you've seen it all, seen the full extent of my evil. You have all the facts before you; whatever you decide about me is fair. I've been out of step with you for a long time, in the wrong since before I was born. What you're after is truth from the inside out. Enter me, then; conceive a new, true life. Soak me in your laundry and I'll come out clean, scrub me and I'll have a snow-white life. Tune me in to foot-tapping songs, set these once-broken bones to dancing. Don't look too close for blemishes, give me a clean bill of health. God, make a fresh start in me, shape a Genesis week from the chaos of my life. Don't throw me out with the trash, or fail to breathe holiness in me. Bring me back from gray exile, put a fresh wind in my sails! Give me a job teaching rebels your ways so the lost can find their way home. Commute my death sentence, God, my salvation God, and I'll sing anthems to your life-giving ways. Unbutton my lips, dear God; I'll let loose with your praise." (Psalm 51:1-15, MSG)

One of the greatest blessings for you as a born-again believer is conversion, which is a change of direction from the world's system to God's system. Conversion is the sinner's response to the conviction of the Holy Spirit. Conversion is the responsive art of two very important words that work together, which are repentance and faith. The Greek word for repent is *metanoia*, which means to have a change of mind, reject sin, follow Christ, and have a desire to learn more of Him. After your mind has been changed, sin has been rejected and your faith will continue to turn you toward God. To turn toward God is to enter into a positive relationship with Him, because He is the anchor of your faith. Repentance should always result in salvation. Let's take a look at the following scripture:

9.   When you believe in Jesus, what will be the result?
"And the keeper of the prison, awaking from sleep and seeing the prison doors open, supposing the prisoners had fled, drew his sword and was about to kill himself. But Paul called with a loud voice, saying, "Do yourself no harm, for we are all here." Then he called for a light, ran in, and fell down trembling before Paul and Silas. And he brought them out and said, "Sirs, what must I do to be saved?" So they said, "Believe on the Lord Jesus Christ, and you will be _____ you and your household." Then they spoke the word of the Lord to him and to all who were in his house. And he took them the same hour of the night and washed their stripes. And immediately he and all his family were baptized. Now when he had brought them into his house, he set food before them; and he rejoiced, having believed in God with all his household." (Acts 16:27-34, NKJV)

THE SALVATION THAT JESUS CAME TO PROVIDE FOR
THE LOST IS DEMONSTRATED IN THE FOLLOWING THREE
PARABLES

1. Who were the two men who went up to the temple to pray

_____ and _____?

"Also He spoke this parable to some who trusted in themselves that they were righteous, and despised others: "Two men went up to the temple to pray, one a _____ and the other a _____ _____. The _____ stood and prayed thus with himself, 'God, I thank You that I am not like other men—extortioners, unjust, adulterers, or even as this tax collector. I fast twice a week; I give tithes of all that I possess.' And the _____ _____ , standing afar off, would not so much as raise his eyes to heaven, but beat his breast, saying, 'God, be merciful to me a sinner!'" (Luke 18:9-13, NKJV)

2. The Lost Sheep, Lost Coin, and Lost Son.

The background of the story is that the publicans and sinners came by the multitudes to hear Jesus, but the Pharisees and scribes began to murmur and complain and criticize Jesus, because He continued to eat with the publicans and sinners. But, His answer to the Pharisees and scribes who complained about Him eating with the publicans and sinners was laid out in three parables, which are:

1. The parable of the lost SHEEP

2. The parable of the lost COIN

3. The parable of the lost SON

Actually, what Jesus was doing was answering with one parable and putting it into three parts, which are three pictures into one frame. We have them in our homes today, two or three or more pictures, but all into one frame known as a *triptych*. What is a triptych? It is a set of three associated artistic, literary, or musical works intended to be appreciated together. This is what Jesus did by describing three parables that really are one that belong together.

3. The following scripture is talking about the Lost _____.
"Then all the tax collectors and the sinners drew near to Him to hear Him. And the Pharisees and scribes complained, saying, "This Man receives sinners and eats with them." So He spoke this parable to them, saying: "What man of you, having a _____ _____ , if he loses one of them, does not leave the ninety-nine in the wilderness, and go after the one which is lost until he finds it? And when he has found it, he lays it on his shoulders, rejoicing. And when he comes home, he calls together his friends and neighbors, saying to them, 'Rejoice with me, for I have found my _____ which was lost!' I say to you that likewise there will be more joy in heaven over one sinner who repents than over ninety-nine just persons who need no repentance." (Luke 15:1-7, NKJV)

4. The following scripture is talking about the Lost _____.
"Or what woman, having _____ _____ _____ if she loses one coin, does not light a lamp, sweep the house, and search carefully until she finds it? And when she has found it, she calls her friends and neighbors together, saying, 'Rejoice with me, for I have found the piece which I lost!' Likewise, I say to you, there is joy in the presence of the angels of God over one sinner who repents." (Luke 15:8-10, NKJV)

5. The following scripture is talking about the Lost _____.

"Then He said: "A certain man had two _____. And the younger of them said to his father, 'Father, give me the portion of goods that falls to me. ' So he divided to them his livelihood. And not many days after, the younger _____ gathered all together, journeyed to a far country, and there wasted his possessions with prodigal living. But when he had spent all, there arose a severe famine in that land, and he began to be in want. Then he went and joined himself to a citizen of that country, and he sent him into his fields to feed swine. And he would gladly have filled his stomach with the pods that the swine ate, and no one gave him anything. "But when he came to himself, he said, 'How many of my father's hired servants have bread enough and to spare, and I perish with hunger! I will arise and go to my father, and will say to him, "Father, I have sinned against heaven and before you, and I am no longer worthy to be called your _____. Make me like one of your hired servants."" "And he arose and came to his father. But when he was still a great way off, his father saw him and had compassion, and ran and fell on his neck and kissed him. And the son said to him, 'Father, I have sinned against heaven and in your sight, and am no longer worthy to be called your _____.' "But the father said to his servants, 'Bring out the best robe and put it on him, and put a ring on his hand and sandals on his feet. And bring the fatted calf here and kill it, and let us eat and be merry; for this my _____ was dead and is alive again; he was _____ and is _____.' And they began to be merry." (Luke 15:11-24. NKJV)

6. Who did Jesus say that He is?
"Then Jesus said to them again, "Most assuredly, I say to you, I am the _____ of the sheep. All who ever came before Me are thieves and robbers, but the sheep did not hear them. I am the _____. If anyone

enters by Me, he will be saved, and will go in and out and find pasture. (John 10:7-9, NKJV)

7. Write the following three things that the thief came to do _____, _____ and _____.
"The thief does not come except to _____, and to _____ and to _____. I have come that they may have life, and that they may have it more abundantly." (John 10:10, NKJV)

8. Jesus came to give _____.
"The thief does not come except to steal, and to kill, and to destroy. I have come that they may have _____, and that they may have it more abundantly." (John 10:10, NKJV)

9. The Good Samaritan.
"Then Jesus answered and said: "A certain man went down from Jerusalem to Jericho, and fell among thieves, who stripped him of his clothing, wounded him, and departed, leaving him half dead. Now by chance a certain priest came down that road. And when he saw him, he passed by on the other side. Likewise a Levite, when he arrived at the place, came and looked, and passed by on the other side. But a certain Samaritan, as he journeyed, came where he was. And when he saw him, he had compassion." (Luke 10:30-33, NKJV)

It's very important that you remember that "conversion" is also the motion of a person toward God or the movement of the soul toward grace and regeneration. It is the infusion of the grace within the soul.

NOTES

2

Spiritually Born

When you become born-again (a believer in Christ) and receive your new nature, your old nature does not die. It is still there and very much alive. There are two natures that are now fighting for possession of the same body which is like two people fighting for the same apartment or home. In Galatians chapter five verse seventeen, your flesh represents the old nature and your spirit represents the new nature.

1.   When you walk in the Spirit, what will you not do?
"I say then: Walk in the Spirit, and you shall not fulfill the _____ of the
_____. For the flesh lusts against the Spirit, and the Spirit against the flesh; and these are contrary to one another, so that you do not do the things that you wish." (Galatians 5:16-17, NKJV)

Apostle Paul went through his own spiritual warfare after his conversion, but through the process, he learned through Jesus Christ how to overcome the flesh. Paul did not just overcome the flesh, but enjoyed the

Holy Spirit reigning in his life. Continue reading the following scriptures to see how Paul went through his own personal process.

"Has then what is good become death to me? Certainly not! But sin, that it might appear sin, was producing death in me through what is good, so that sin through the commandment might become exceedingly sinful. For we know that the law is spiritual, but I am carnal, sold under sin. For what I am doing, I do not understand. For what I will to do, that I do not practice; but what I hate, that I do. If, then, I do what I will not to do, I agree with the law that it is good. But now, it is no longer I who do it, but sin that dwells in me. For I know that in me (that is, in my flesh) nothing good dwells; for to will is present with me, but how to perform what is good I do not find. For the good that I will to do, I do not do; but the evil I will not to do, that I practice. Now if I do what I will not to do, it is no longer I who do it, but sin that dwells in me. I find then a law, that evil is present with me, the one who wills to do good. For I delight in the law of God according to the inward man. But I see another law in my members, warring against the law of my mind, and bringing me into captivity to the law of sin which is in my members. O wretched man that I am! Who will deliver me from this body of death? I thank God— through Jesus Christ our Lord! So then, with the mind I myself serve the law of God, but with the flesh the law of sin." (Romans 7:13-25. NKJV)

The entire chapter of Romans chapter eight is a very encouraging chapter on how Paul let the Holy Spirit reign in his life.

"There is therefore now no condemnation to those who are in Christ Jesus, who do not walk according to the flesh, but according to the Spirit. For the law of the Spirit of life in Christ Jesus has made me free from the law of sin and death. For what the law could not do in that it was weak through the flesh, God did by sending His own Son in the likeness of sinful flesh, on account of sin: He condemned sin in the flesh, that the righteous requirement of the law might be fulfilled in us who do not walk according to the flesh but according to the Spirit. For those who live according to the flesh set their minds on the things of the flesh, but those who live according to the Spirit, the things of the Spirit. For to be carnally minded is death, but to be spiritually minded is life and peace. Because the carnal mind is enmity against God; for it is not subject to the law of God, nor indeed can be. So then, those who are in the flesh cannot please God. But you are not in the flesh but in the Spirit, if indeed the Spirit of God dwells in you. Now if anyone does not have the Spirit of Christ, he is not His. And if Christ is in you, the body is dead because of sin, but the Spirit is life because of righteousness. But if the Spirit of Him who raised Jesus from the dead dwells in you, He who raised Christ from the dead will also give life to your mortal bodies through His Spirit who dwells in you. Therefore, brethren, we are debtors—not to the flesh, to live according to the flesh. For if you live according to the flesh you will die; but if by the Spirit you put to death the deeds of the body, you will live. For as many as are led by the Spirit of God, these are sons of God. For you did not receive the spirit of bondage again to fear, but you received the Spirit of adoption by whom we cry out, "Abba, Father." The Spirit Himself bears witness with our spirit that we are children of God, and if children, then heirs—heirs of God and joint heirs with Christ, if indeed we suffer with Him, that we may also be glorified together. For I consider that the sufferings of this present time are not worthy to be compared with the glory which shall be revealed in us. For the earnest expectation of the creation eagerly waits for the revealing of the sons of God. For the creation was subjected to futility, not willingly, but because of Him who subjected it in hope; because the creation itself also will be delivered from the bondage of corruption into the glorious liberty of the children of God. For we know that the whole creation groans and labors with birth pangs together until now. Not only that, but we also who have the firstfruits of the Spirit, even we ourselves groan within ourselves, eagerly waiting for the adoption, the redemption of our body. For we were saved in this hope, but hope that is seen is not hope; for why does one still hope for what he sees? But if we hope for what we do not see, we eagerly wait for it with perseverance. Likewise the Spirit also helps in our weaknesses. For we do not know what we should pray for as we ought, but the Spirit Himself makes intercession for us with groanings which cannot be uttered. Now He who searches the hearts knows what the mind of the Spirit is, because He makes intercession for the saints according to the will of God. And we know that all things work together for good to those who love God, to those who are the called according to His purpose. For whom He foreknew, He also predestined to be con-formed to the image of His Son, that He might be the firstborn among many brethren. Moreover whom He predestined, these He also called; whom He called, these He also justified; and whom He justified, these He also glorified. What then shall we say to these things? If God is for us, who can be against us? He who did not spare His own Son, but delivered Him up for us all, how shall He not with Him also freely give us all things? Who shall bring a charge against God's elect? It is God who justifies. Who is he who condemns? It is Christ who died, and furthermore is also risen, who is even at the right hand of God, who also makes intercession for us. Who shall separate us from the love of Christ? Shall tribulation, or distress, or persecution, or famine, or nakedness, or peril, or sword? As it is written: "For Your sake we are killed all day long; We are accounted as sheep for the slaughter." Yet in all these things we are more than conquerors through Him who loved us. For I am persuaded that neither death nor life, nor angels nor principalities nor powers, nor things present nor things to come, nor height nor depth, nor any other created thing, shall be able to separate us from the love of God which is in Christ Jesus our Lord." (Romans 8:1-39, NKJV)

2. What should a believer in Christ not have confidence in?

3. Do not have any confidence in your _____ .
"Finally, my fellow believers, continue to rejoice and delight in the LORD. To write the same things again is no trouble for me, and it is a safeguard for you. Look out for the dogs [the Judaizers, the legalists], look out for the troublemakers, look out for the false circumcision [those who claim circumcision is necessary for salvation]; for we [who are born-again have been reborn from above--spiritually transformed, renewed, set apart for His purpose and] are the true circumcision, who worship in the Spirit of God and glory and take pride and exult in Christ Jesus and place no confidence [in what we have or who we are] in the flesh—though I myself might have [some grounds for] confidence in the _____ [if I were pursuing salvation by works]. If anyone else thinks that he has reason to be confident in the _____ [that is, in his own efforts to achieve salvation], I have far more:" (Philippians 3:1-4, AMP)

4. Feed your spirit, which is the new nature.
"Therefore, laying aside all malice, all deceit, hypocrisy, envy, and all evil speaking, as newborn babes, desire the pure milk of the word, that you may grow thereby," (I Peter 2:1-2, NKJV)

"So clean house! Make a clean sweep of malice and pretense, envy and hurtful talk. You've had a taste of God. Now, like infants at the breast, drink deep of God's pure kindness. Then you'll grow up mature and whole in God." (I Peter 2:1-3, MSG)

5. Starve the flesh, which is the old nature.
"Let us conduct ourselves properly and honorably as in the [light of] day, not in carousing and drunkenness, not in sexual promiscuity and irresponsibility, not in quarreling and jealousy. But clothe yourselves with the Lord Jesus Christ, and make no provision for [nor even think about gratifying] the flesh in regard to its improper desires." (Romans13:13-14, AMP)

The starvation of the flesh can only become alive again if you start to feed it, because it is never dead, it's just in starvation mode. If you start to feed your flesh again, I will guarantee you this, it will recover its strength and give you trouble.

"Everything is permissible for me, but not all things are beneficial. Everything is permissible for me, but I will not be enslaved by anything [and brought under its power, allowing it to control me]." (I Corinthians 6:12, AMP)

"Just because something is technically legal doesn't mean that it's spiritually appropriate. If I went around doing whatever I thought I could get by with, I'd be a slave to my whims." (I Corinthians 6:12, MSG)

The reason why you can see and hear about many born-again believers that have lived consecrated spiritual lives and suddenly fall from grace is because they have yielded to an unguarded moment in their lives to some former habit of the old fleshly nature.

6.   You cannot feed your flesh and sprit nature at the same time. "No one can serve two masters; for either he will hate the one and love the other, or he will be devoted to the one and despise the other. You cannot serve God and mammon [money, possessions, fame, status, or whatever is valued more than the Lord]." (Matthew 6:24, AMP)

"You can't worship two gods at once. Loving one god, you'll end up hating the other. Adoration of one feeds contempt for the other. You can't worship God and Money both." (Matthew 6:24, MSG)

7.   As a believer in Jesus, what is the result of hanging around bad company?
"Do not be deceived: "Evil company corrupts _____ _____." (I Corinthians 15:33, NKJV)

"Do not be so deceived and misled! Evil companionships (communion, associations) corrupt and deprave good manners and morals and character." (I Corinthians 15:33, AMPC)

8.   Don't allow your flesh to speak.
"Let there be no filthiness (obscenity, indecency) nor foolish and sinful (silly and corrupt) talk, nor coarse jesting, which are not fitting or becoming; but instead voice your thankfulness [to God]." (Ephesians 5:4, AMPC)

"Don't allow love to turn into lust, setting off a downhill slide into sexual promiscuity, filthy practices, or bullying greed. Though some tongues just love the taste of gossip, those who follow Jesus have better uses for language than that. Don't talk dirty or silly. That kind of talk doesn't fit our style. Thanksgiving is our dialect." (Ephesians 5:3-4, MSG)

THREE WAYS TO OVERCOME THE FLESH

1. Amputation.

If your hands cause you to steal, stop; if your feet start to take ungodly steps, stop; and if your eyes start to lust after someone or something... STOP!!!

"So if your hand or foot causes you to sin, cut it off and throw it away. It's better to enter eternal life with only one hand or one foot than to be thrown into eternal fire with both of your hands and feet. And if your eye causes you to sin, gouge it out and throw it away. It's better to enter eternal life with only one eye than to have two eyes and be thrown into the fire of hell." (Matthew 18:8-9, NLT)

2. Mortification.

"Therefore put to death your members which are on the earth: fornication, uncleanness, passion, evil desire, and covetousness, which is idolatry. Because of these things the wrath of God is coming upon the sons of disobedience, in which you yourselves once walked when you lived in them. But now you yourselves are to put off all these: anger, wrath, malice, blasphemy, filthy language out of your mouth. Do not lie to one another, since you have put off the old man with his deeds, and have put on the new man who is renewed in knowledge according to the image of Him who created him," (Colossians 3:5-10, NKJV)

There are some things in your life that cannot be amputated, but they have to be removed in another way, which is called mortification. These are the things in your life that take time to overcome such as weak nerves, impatience, pride, and more. The difference between amputation and mortification is that amputation is an external process and mortification is an internal process. It is allowing God to do the work within you.

3.   What is it a believer is supposed to work out _____.
"Therefore, my beloved, as you have always obeyed, not as in my presence only, but now much more in my absence, work out your own _____ with _____ and _____; for it is God who works in you both to will and to do for His good pleasure." (Philippians 2:12-13, NKJV)

"What I'm getting at, friends, is that you should simply keep on doing what you've done from the beginning. When I was living among you, you lived in responsive obedience. Now that I'm separated from you, keep it up. Better yet, redouble your efforts. Be energetic in your life of salvation, reverent and sensitive before God. That energy is God's energy, an energy deep within you, God himself willing and working at what will give him the most pleasure." (Philippians 2:12-13, MSG)

4.   Limitation.
Write the two things a believer should lay aside? _____ and _____.

"Therefore we also, since we are surrounded by so great a cloud of witnesses, let us lay aside every _____ , and the _____ which so easily ensnares us, and let us run with endurance the race that is set before us," (Hebrews 12:1, NKJV)

There is a difference between weights and sins. All weights are not sins, but all sins are weights. Doing too much work on your job can be a weight in your life but not going to work can be a sin, which will eventually be a weight.

5. If you know to do good but refuse to do it, what is it called? "Therefore, to him who knows to do good and does not do it, to him it is _____." (James 4:17, NKJV)

"For we hear that there are some who walk among you in a disorderly manner, not working at all, but are busybodies. Now those who are such we command and exhort through our Lord Jesus Christ that they work in quietness and eat their own bread." (II Thessalonians 3:11-12, NKJV)

"Don't you remember the rule we had when we lived with you? "If you don't work, you don't eat." And now we're getting reports that a bunch of lazy good-for-nothings are taking advantage of you. This must not be tolerated. We command them to get to work immediately—no excuses, no arguments—and earn their own keep. Friends, don't slack off in doing your duty." (II Thessalonians 3:10-13, MSG)

Remember that your flesh represents the old nature and your spirit represents the new nature. You cannot get rid of your old nature until the death of your fleshly body. Always remember that spiritual warfare

62

between your flesh and spirit will continue until Jesus comes, but as you continue to yield to the Spirit, you will always come out victorious!

NOTES

3

The Standing of a Believer

There are three classes of professing born-again believers.

1. There a born-again believers that are saved and know it.

2. There are born-again believers that are saved and not sure of it.

3. There are people that are not saved, but think they are.

Most born-again believers when asked the question, "are you saved" will respond with answers, such as "I hope so" or "I think I am". Some born-again believers will even get an attitude by turning a question into a question buy responding with a statement, such as "are you," while other believers think the positive answer is to say, "We will never know until we die."

The major reason that many born-again believers are not really sure if they are saved is because they do not know how to distinguish between two major topics: the standing as a believer and the state as a believer. The only way for any believer to learn about the believer standing is through the Word of God. The believer's standing is the standing of a son. You become a son of God when you receive Him as Savior.

"But as many as received Him, to them He gave the right to become children of God, to those who believe in His name: who were born, not of blood, nor of the will of the flesh, nor of the will of man, but of God." (John 1:12-13, NKJV)

The Gospel only benefits the people who have received Jesus into their heart and have activated their delegated power to use their liberty and right to be saved, according to their will.

1. How many people does God want to be saved?
"For this is good and acceptable in the sight of God our Savior, who desires _____ men to be saved and to come to the knowledge of the truth. For there is one God and one Mediator between God and men, the Man Christ Jesus," (I Timothy 2:3-5, NKJV)

"Don't overlook the obvious here, friends. With God, one day is as good as a thousand years, a thousand years as a day. God isn't late with his promise as some measure lateness. He is restraining himself on account of you, holding back the End because he doesn't want anyone lost. He's giving everyone space and time to change." (II Peter 3:8-9, MSG)

A person who has not received Jesus as Savior cannot be one of His, because the scripture declares His sheep will hear His voice. There are three things that every born-again believer needs to continue to receive eternal life.

    2.   Every believer must continue to believe, which means that it is very important to have complete and continued obedience and _____ in _____.

"For by grace you have been saved through _____ and that not of yourselves; it is the gift of God, not of works, lest anyone should boast." (Ephesians 2:8-9, NKJV)

"For in it the righteousness of God is revealed from _____ to ____; as it is written, "The just shall live by _____ ." (Romans 1:17, NKJV)

"I have been crucified with Christ; it is no longer I who live, but Christ lives in me; and the life which I now live in the flesh I live by _____ in the Son of God, who loved me and gave Himself for me." (Galatians 2:20, NKJV)

"Now the just shall live by _____; But if anyone draws back, My soul has no pleasure in him." (Hebrews 10:38, NKJV)

    3.   Every believer must continue to hear God's _____.

"Most assuredly, I say to you, he who does not enter the sheepfold by the door, but climbs up some other way, the same is a thief and a robber. But he who enters by the door is the shepherd of the sheep. To him the doorkeeper opens, and the sheep hear his _____; and he calls his own sheep by name and leads them out. And when he brings out his own sheep, he goes before them; and the sheep follow him, for they know his _____. Yet they will by no means follow a stranger, but will flee from him, for they do not know the _____ of strangers." Jesus used this illustration, but they did not understand the things which He spoke to them." (John 10:1-6, NKJV)

It is very possible for you to have ears connected to your head, but not hear what is being said.

"Therefore I speak to them in parables, because seeing they do not see, and hearing they do not hear, nor do they understand." (Matthew 13:13, NKJV)

It is not that a person cannot see or hear the right things to do; they just refuse to see or hear what is being said. Most people are capable of understanding, but refuse to accept the truth. But, the Bible says in John chapter eight verses thirty-one to thirty-two:

"Then Jesus said to those Jews who believed Him, "If you abide in My word, you are My disciples indeed. And you shall know the truth, and the truth shall make you free." (John 8:31-32, NKJV)

4. Jesus said when we abide in His "Word" what are we?

5. Jesus said once we know the truth what will happen?

"Then Jesus said to those Jews who believed Him, "If you abide in My word, you are My _____ indeed. (John 8:31, NKJV)

6. When you know the truth what will happened?

"And you shall know the truth, and the truth shall _____ _____
_____." (John 8:32, NKJV)

God gave you two ears and one mouth, so you can listen as twice as much as you talk.

"Understand this, my beloved brothers and sisters. Let everyone be quick to hear [be a careful, thoughtful listener], slow to speak [a speaker of carefully chosen words and], slow to anger [patient, reflective, forgiving];" (James 1:19, AMP)

It is very important to realize that faith alone will save you, but the faith that saves is not alone. Faith produces once you receive Jesus into your heart. It is the consistency or the continuing in the truth that will make you free. Any believer that is active in their local church through works and not interested in the Word of God is an active human time-bomb and is very dangerous to the local church.

MARY AND MARTHA WORSHIPPED AND SERVED

1. What was Martha's problem after she accepted Jesus into her house? _____ _____ _____

"Now it happened as they went that He entered a certain village; and a certain woman named Martha welcomed Him into her house. And she had a sister called Mary, who also sat at Jesus' feet and heard His word. But Martha was _____ with much serving, and she approached Him and said, "Lord, do You not care that my sister has left me to serve alone? Therefore tell her to help me." And Jesus answered and said to her, "Martha, Martha, you are _____ and _____ about many things. But one thing is needed, and Mary has chosen that good part, which will not be taken away from her." (Luke 10:38-42, NKJV)

Don't be a busy believer that cannot stop being a busybody long enough to hear God's Word for your life.

2. God wants us to be _____ of the Word, and not _____ only.

"But be _____ of the Word, and not _____ only, deceiving yourselves." (James 1:22, NKJV)

"Don't fool yourself into thinking that you are a listener when you are anything but, letting the Word go in one ear and out the other. Act on what you hear! Those who hear and don't act are like those who glance in the mirror, walk away, and two minutes later have no idea who they are, what they look like." (James 1:22-24. MSG)

When the Scripture says to "be doers of the Word and not hearers only" requires the attention of every believer to be active. You can read about history in your history books, but it will ask you to do nothing. You can study science, but it will not make a demand on you. You can look at a cookbook and read the recipe, but it does not tell you that you have to cook. The Word of God is a command; it is an appeal to action. There is a difference between being a student in the class and auditing the class. Students that are auditing the class never had to take exams, make preparations for the exam, never wrote any papers, and did not get a diploma. People that are auditors just sit there, but a student that is enrolled in class is not just a hearer, but a doer.

3. Every believer must continue to be a _____ of Jesus Christ.

As a born-again believer, you have to continue your walk of faith not just in the beginning, but daily throughout your life.

"My sheep hear My voice, and I know them, and they _____ Me. (John 10:27, NKJV)

4. Jesus said when we follow Him, that He will give us _____ _____.

"And I give them _____ _____, and they shall never perish; neither shall anyone snatch them out of My hand." (John 10:28, NKJV)

As a born-again believer, you will never perish as long as you continue to meet the conditions. God cannot keep anyone that does not want to be kept or doing the opposite of God's Word and will for their life.

NOTES

_____

_____

_____

_____

_____

_____

_____

_____

4

The State of a Believer

According to the Scriptures in the Word of God, the *standing* of a believer is settled and sure, but the *state* of a believer is variable. The word variable is something that is changeable and before you become a believer in Christ, you only had to deal with one nature, but the moment that you receive Jesus into your heart, another nature was birthed into your life. It's not that you have lost your old Adam or fleshly nature when you received the new Adam, which is the spiritual nature. What the first Adam could not do, the second Adam (JESUS) did. John the third chapter and six verse says,

1. That which is _____ of the _____ is _____, and that which is born of the _____ is _____." (John 3:6, NKJV)

Now, God does not intend to change the flesh, which is the old Adam nature you still have, because the fact of the matter is that the old nature cannot be changed. Your old nature it's always at war with God. Why? The following scripture tells us:

2. What is the carnal mind against God?

"Because the carnal mind is _____ against God; for it is not subject to the law of God, nor indeed can be." (Romans 8:7, NKJV)

3. What does the Word of God say you can't do in the flesh?

_____ _____

"So then, those who are in the flesh cannot please God." (Romans 8:8, NKJV)

"Those who think they can do it on their own end up obsessed with measuring their own moral muscle but never get around to exercising it in real life. Those who trust God's action in them find that God's Spirit is in them—living and breathing God! Obsession with self in these matters is a dead end; attention to God leads us out into the open, into a spacious, free life. Focusing on the self is the opposite of focusing on God. Anyone completely absorbed in self ignores God, ends up thinking more about self than God. That person ignores who God is and what he is doing. And God isn't pleased at being ignored." (Romans 8:5-8, MSG)

Whenever you do and obey the things of the flesh, it becomes enmity with God. This type of yielding to the flesh will never obey the law of God, because it submits to sin and whenever your flesh stops rebelling, it will stop sinning. As a believer, you have a dual nature and depending on which nature is supreme, will show what type of individual you really are.

"No one who is born of God [deliberately, knowingly, and habitually] practices sin, because God's seed [His principle of life, the essence of His righteous character] remains [permanently] in him [who is born again--who is reborn from above--spiritually transformed, renewed, and set apart for His purpose]; and he [who is born again] cannot habitually [live a life characterized by] sin, because he is born of God and longs to please Him." (I John 3:9, AMP)

"People conceived and brought into life by God don't make a practice of sin. How could they? God's seed is deep within them, making them who they are. It's not in the nature of the God-begotten to practice and parade sin. Here's how you tell the difference between God's children and the Devil's children: The one who won't practice righteous ways isn't from God, nor is the one who won't love brother or sister. A simple test." (I John 3:9-10, MSG)

As a born-again believer, you have been given a new nature and this nature does not and will not commit sin. When the Scripture says that "whosoever is born of God does not commit sin" it is not implying one act of sin, but it talks about you not living or practicing in sin.

"My little children (believers, dear ones), I am writing you these things so that you will not sin and violate God's law. And if anyone sins, we have an Advocate [who will intercede for us] with the Father: Jesus Christ the righteous [the upright, the just One, who conforms to the Father's will in every way--purpose, thought, and action]." (I John 2:1, AMP)

When the Scripture says anyone, it is not just talking literally about any person, but it is talking about a born-again believer, a person that has received Jesus Christ. As a believer you will sin, but you should not practice sin. But if you sin, the Bible says that you have an advocate with the Father. John makes it very clear that it is God's will that we live without sin. As a born-again believer, you will not sin as long as you walk in the light, but if you start focusing on the darkness of your life and fall into sin, you can still have hope and confess your sin and be cleansed again.

4. If we walk in the light, what will we have with each other?

5. How much sin will the blood of Jesus cleanse us from?

6. When we confess our sins, what will Jesus do?

"But if we walk in the light as He is in the light, we have _____ with one another, and the blood of Jesus Christ His Son cleanses us from _____ sin. If we say that we have no sin, we deceive ourselves, and the truth is not in us. If we confess our sins, He is faithful and just to _____ us our sins and to _____ us from all _____ . If we say that we have not sinned, we make Him a liar, and His word is not in us." (I John 1:7-10, NKJV)

"If we claim that we experience a shared life with him and continue to stumble around in the dark, we're obviously lying through our teeth— we're not living what we claim. But if we walk in the light, God himself being the light, we also experience a shared life with one another, as the sacrificed blood of Jesus, God's Son, purges all our sin.

76

If we claim that we're free of sin, we're only fooling ourselves. A claim like that is errant nonsense. On the other hand, if we admit our sins— make a clean breast of them—he won't let us down; he'll be true to himself. He'll forgive our sins and purge us of all wrongdoing. If we claim that we've never sinned, we out-and-out contradict God—make a liar out of him. A claim like that only shows off our ignorance of God." (I John 1:6-10, MSG)

The important thing that I want you to notice is in verse seven when it says, "If we walk in the light." The scripture does not say if you walk according to the light, but if you walk in the light. It is possible to walk in darkness and think you are alright, until the light comes on and you find yourself in a place where you do not belong. You cannot have fellowship with God while you are living (practicing) in sin.

When you confess your sins, it's from the Greek word *homologeo* which means to say the same thing. *Logeo* means "to say" and *homo* means "the same". As a born-again believer, you are supposed to say the same thing that God says. If God says what you were doing is sin, then you are supposed to be like a parrot and say, "Yes, Lord it is sin," because confessing your sins is to say the same thing that God says. After your sin or sins are confessed, then God will come in and cleanse you.

Paul had labor and prevailed in preaching in prayer for the Galatians and when they had fallen, Paul found himself traveling again until they would come back to God and Christ be formed in them again. They had fallen from grace and had to be renewed in Christ again. The Greek word *palin* means "again," once more. It refers to something which could not be done again if it had not been done once before.

7.   When a believer sins, what do they have with the Father?
"My little children, these things I write to you, so that you may not sin. And if anyone sins, we have an _____ with the Father, _____ _____ the righteous." I John 2:1, NKJV

Christ is a *parakletos* to a born-again believer, which means one called to the side of another for help or counsel. The Spirit is your *Paraclete*, or helper, on earth and Christ is the *Paraclete*, or helper, in heaven.

"We know that whoever is born of God does not sin; but he who has been born of God keeps himself, and the wicked one does not touch him." (I John 5:18, NKJV)

This scripture means that if you are born of God, you do not practice sin. Remember, the prodigal son did not stay in the pigpen; he got up and left, because he realized that he was not a pig, but his son.

"For there is not a just man on earth who does good And does not sin." (Ecclesiastes 7:20, NKJV)

"… for all have sinned and fall short of the glory of God," (Romans 3:23, NKJV)

"Therefore, to him who knows to do good and does not do it, to him it is sin." (James 4:17, NKJV)

78

NOTES

5

The Carnal-Minded Believer

There are four types of people in the Bible when speaking on the topic of salvation, as it pertains to a born-again believer. The four types are as follows: carnal-minded believer, spiritual-minded believer, natural person, and the apostate person. In first Corinthians chapter two verse fourteen through chapter three verse three, it identifies three types, which are natural, spiritual, and carnal. Matthew chapter seven verse twenty-one to twenty-three talks about the apostate person:

1. Can the natural man receive the things of the Spirit of God? NO/YES (Circle)

2. Why can't the natural man know the Spirit of God?
"But the natural man _____ _____ receive the things of the Spirit of God, for they are foolishness to him; nor can he know them, because they are _____ _____. But he who is spiritual judges all things, yet he himself is rightly judged by no one. For "who has known the mind of the LORD that he may instruct Him?" But we have the mind of Christ." (I Corinthians 2:14-16, NKJV)

"And I, brethren, could not speak to you as to spiritual people but as to carnal, as to babes in Christ. I fed you with milk and not with solid food; for until now you were not able to receive it, and even now you are still not able; for you are still carnal. For where there are envy, strife, and divisions among you, are you not carnal and behaving like mere men?" (I Corinthians 3:1-3, NKJV)

CARNAL-MINDED BELIEVER

You cannot be a carnal Christian, but you can be a believer with the carnal mindset in your thoughts. The carnal-minded believer is born-again, just like the spiritual-minded believer, but they are not growing in the Word of God and continue to struggle with their fleshly desires, which can eventually lead to sin. James chapter one verse thirteen says,

1. Does temptation come from God? NO/YES (Circle)

2. How are we tempted?
"Let no one say when he is tempted, "I am being tempted by God" [for _____ does not _____ from _____, but from our own flaws]; for God cannot be tempted by [what is] evil, and He Himself tempts no one. But each one is tempted when he is _____ away, _____ and _____ [to commit sin] by his _____ [worldly] _____ (lust, passion)." (James 1:13-14, AMP)

Without the willingness of obedience to the Word of God, the carnal-minded believer will eventually not be a disciple of Christ at all. The carnal mind of a believer is not like the natural person, because the natural person is not born-again and the natural person is not like the

GO|STOP SALVATION

apostate person who has a form of godliness, but lacks power. They both look like the spiritual-minded person in motion and deed and once were born-again, but have totally left the biblical teachings of Christ to serve something or someone else.

"… having a form of godliness but denying its power. And from such people turn away!" (II Timothy 3:5, NKJV)

"Don't be naive. There are difficult times ahead. As the end approaches, people are going to be self-absorbed, money-hungry, self-promoting, stuck-up, profane, contemptuous of parents, crude, coarse, dog-eat-dog, unbending, slanderers, impulsively wild, savage, cynical, treacherous, ruthless, bloated windbags, addicted to lust, and allergic to God. They'll make a show of religion, but behind the scenes they're animals. Stay clear of these people." (II Timothy 3:1-5, MSG)

The Bible makes it very clear that you cannot serve two God's.

3.   As a believer in Jesus, can you serve two Gods? NO/YES (Circle)

"No one can serve two masters; for either he will hate the one and love the other, or else he will be loyal to the one and despise the other. You cannot serve God and mammon." (Matthew 6:24, NKJV)

"You shall have no other gods before Me." (Deuteronomy 5:7, NKJV)

In Romans, Paul uses the phrase "or body of sin might be done away."

83

"We know that our old self [our human nature without the Holy Spirit] was nailed to the cross with Him, in order that our body of sin might be done away with, so that we would no longer be slaves to sin. For the person who has died [with Christ] has been freed from [the power of] sin." (Romans 6:6-7, AMP)

The Greek word for destroyed is *katargeo*, which means that it will be inactive, made of no effect, paralyzed, canceled, or unemployed, or do away. When you become a born-again believer, sin is no longer your master, but that does not mean that you will not be tempted to sin. It does mean that you now have the power to have dominion over your sins. The Corinthian's were born-again believers with a carnal mentality.

"Paul, called to be an apostle of Jesus Christ through the will of God, and Sosthenes our brother, To the church of God which is at Corinth, to those who are sanctified in Christ Jesus, called to be saints, with all who in every place call on the name of Jesus Christ our Lord, both theirs and ours: Grace to you and peace from God our Father and the Lord Jesus Christ. I thank my God always concerning you for the grace of God which was given to you by Christ Jesus, that you were enriched in everything by Him in all utterance and all knowledge, even as the testimony of Christ was confirmed in you, so that you come short in no gift, eagerly waiting for the revelation of our Lord Jesus Christ, who will also confirm you to the end, that you may be blameless in the day of our Lord Jesus Christ. God is faithful, by whom you were called into the fellowship of His Son, Jesus Christ our Lord." (I Corinthians 1:1-9, NKJV)

They were gifted, but they operated it in the flesh. The carnal-minded Corinthian's had two natures just like the spiritual man, but had allowed their old nature to dominate their new nature. Most of the time, it is very hard to tell the difference from a believer with a carnal mentality compared to an unbeliever with no biblical mentality toward God. A good example of this is located in Genesis chapters thirteen and nineteen regarding the story of Lot. It is very possible to come to the conclusion that Lot was a lost man. Let's now take a look at these chapters:

"Then Abram went up from Egypt, he and his wife and all that he had, and Lot with him, to the South. Abram was very rich in livestock, in silver, and in gold. And he went on his journey from the South as far as Bethel, to the place where his tent had been at the beginning, between Bethel and Ai, to the place of the altar which he had made there at first. And there Abram called on the name of the LORD. Lot also, who went with Abram, had flocks and herds and tents. Now the land was not able to support them, that they might dwell together, for their possessions were so great that they could not dwell together. And there was strife between the herdsmen of Abram's livestock and the herdsmen of Lot's livestock. The Canaanites and the Perizzites then dwelt in the land. So Abram said to Lot, "Please let there be no strife between you and me, and between my herdsmen and your herdsmen; for we are brethren. Is not the whole land before you? Please separate from me. If you take the left, then I will go to the right; or, if you go to the right, then I will go to the left." And Lot lifted his eyes and saw all the plain of Jordan, that it was well watered everywhere (before the LORD destroyed Sodom and Gomorrah) like the garden of the LORD, like the land of Egypt as you go toward Zoar. Then Lot chose for himself all the plain of Jordan, and Lot journeyed east. And they separated from each other. Abram dwelt in the land of Canaan, and Lot dwelt in the cities of the plain and pitched his tent even as far as Sodom. But the men of Sodom were exceedingly wicked and sinful against the LORD. And the LORD said to Abram, after Lot had separated from him: "Lift your eyes now and look from the place where you are—northward, southward, eastward, and westward; for all the land which you see I give to you and your descendants forever. And I will make your descendants as the dust of the earth; so that if a man could number the dust of the earth, then your descendants also could be numbered. Arise, walk in the land through its length and its width, for I give it to you." Then Abram moved his tent, and went and dwelt by the terebinth trees of Mamre, which are in Hebron, and built an altar there to the LORD." (Genesis 13:1-18, NKJV)

"Now the two angels came to Sodom in the evening, and Lot was sitting in the gate of Sodom. When Lot saw them, he rose to meet them, and he bowed himself with his face toward the ground. And he said, "Here now, my lords, please turn in to your servant's house and spend the night, and wash your feet; then you may rise early and go on your way." And they said, "No, but we will spend the night in the open square." But he insisted strongly; so they turned in to him and entered his house. Then he made them a feast, and baked unleavened bread, and they ate. Now before they lay down, the men of the city, the men of Sodom, both old and young, all the people from every quarter, surrounded the house. And they called to Lot and said to him, "Where are the men who came to you tonight? Bring them out to us that we may know them carnally." So Lot went out to them through the doorway, shut the door behind him, and said, "Please, my brethren, do not do so wickedly! See now, I have two daughters who have not known a man; please, let me bring them out to you, and you may do to them as you wish; only do nothing to these men, since this is the reason they have come under the shadow of my roof." And they said, "Stand back!" Then they said, "This one came in to stay here, and he keeps acting as a judge; now we will deal worse with you than with them." So they pressed hard against the man Lot, and came near to break down the door. But the men reached out their hands and pulled Lot into the house with them, and shut the door. And they struck the men who were at the doorway of the house with blindness, both small and great, so that they became weary trying to find the door. Then the men said to Lot, "Have you anyone else here? Son-in-law, your sons, your daughters, and whomever you have in the city— take them out of this place! For we will destroy this place, because the outcry against them has grown great before the face of the LORD, and the LORD has sent us to destroy it." So Lot went out and spoke to his sons-in-law, who had married his daughters, and said, "Get up, get out of this place; for the LORD will destroy this city!" But to his sons-in-law he seemed to be joking. When the morning dawned, the angels urged Lot to hurry, saying, "Arise, take your wife and your two daughters who are here, lest you be consumed in the punishment of the city." And while he lingered, the men took hold of his hand, his wife's hand, and the hands of his two daughters, the LORD being merciful to him, and they brought him out and set him outside the city. So it came to pass, when they had brought them outside, that he said, "Escape for your life! Do not look behind you nor stay anywhere in the plain. Escape to the mountains, lest you be destroyed." Then Lot said to them, "Please, no, my lords! Indeed now, your servant has found favor in your sight, and you have increased your mercy which you have shown me by saving my life; but I cannot escape to the mountains, lest some evil overtake me and I die. See now, this city is near enough to flee to, and it is a little one; please let me escape there (is it not a little one?) and my soul shall live." And he said to him, "See,

I have favored you concerning this thing also, in that I will not over-throw this city for which you have spoken. Hurry, escape there. For I cannot do anything until you arrive there." Therefore the name of the city was called Zoar. The sun had risen upon the earth when Lot entered Zoar. Then the LORD rained brimstone and fire on Sodom and Gomor-rah, from the LORD out of the heavens. So He overthrew those cities, all the plain, all the inhabitants of the cities, and what grew on the ground. But his wife looked back behind him, and she became a pillar of salt. And Abraham went early in the morning to the place where he had stood before the LORD. Then he looked toward Sodom and Gomorrah, and toward all the land of the plain; and he saw, and behold, the smoke of the land which went up like the smoke of a furnace. And it came to pass, when God destroyed the cities of the plain, that God remembered Abraham, and sent Lot out of the midst of the overthrow, when He overthrew the cities in which Lot had dwelt. Then Lot went up out of Zoar and dwelt in the mountains, and his two daughters were with him; for he was afraid to dwell in Zoar. And he and his two daughters dwelt in a cave. Now the firstborn said to the younger, "Our father is old, and there is no man on the earth to come in to us as is the custom of all the earth. Come, let us make our father drink wine, and we will lie with him, that we may preserve the lineage of our father." So they made their father drink wine that night. And the firstborn went in and lay with her father, and he did not know when she lay down or when she arose. It happened on the next day that the firstborn said to the younger, "Indeed I lay with my father last night; let us make him drink wine tonight also, and you go in and lie with him, that we may preserve the lineage of our father." Then they made their father drink wine that night also. And the younger arose and lay with him, and he did not know when she lay down or when she arose. Thus both the daughters of Lot were with child by their father. The firstborn bore a son and called his name Moab; he is the father of the Moabites to this day. And the younger, she also bore a son and called his name Ben-Ammi; he is the father of the people of Ammon to this day." (Genesis 19:1-38, NKJV)

Now, let's take a look at second Peter chapter two verse seven...

"… and delivered righteous Lot, who was oppressed by the filthy conduct of the wicked." (II Peter 2:7, NKJV)

The preceding scriptures let us know that Lot was a righteous man, but had a carnal mentality. The only way to be delivered from a carnal mentality as a believer is by the cross. Jesus died on the cross to cleanse us from all our sins that we have committed, past, present and future, but you have to accept Jesus Christ as your Lord and Savior to be saved from the sin nature of carnal mentality. To become a believer in Jesus Christ only takes a few seconds, but sanctification and the deliverance from our carnal mentality nature is a daily process.

4.   When we follow Jesus what three things did He tell us to do?

_____ _____ _____

"Then He said to them all, "If anyone desires to come after Me, let him _____ himself, and take up his _____ daily, and _____ Me." (Luke 9:23, NKJV)

The following scriptures are to inform you that the power over temptation has already been given to you as a born-again believer in Christ.

5. God will not _____ you.

"Let no one say when he is tempted, "I am tempted by God"; for God _____ be _____ by evil, nor does He Himself tempt anyone." (James 1:13, NKJV)

"Don't let anyone under pressure to give in to evil say, "God is trying to trip me up." God is impervious to evil, and puts evil in no one's way. The temptation to give in to evil comes from us and only us. We have no one to blame but the leering, seducing flare-up of our own lust. Lust gets pregnant, and has a baby: sin! Sin grows up to adulthood, and becomes a real killer." (James 1:13-15, MSG)

6. God provided you a way to _____ temptation.
"No temptation has overtaken you except such as is common to man; but God is faithful, who will not allow you to be tempted beyond what you are able, but with the _____ will also make the way of _____ that you may be able to bear it." (I Corinthians 10:13, NKJV)

"No test or temptation that comes your way is beyond the course of what others have had to face. All you need to remember is that God will never let you down; he'll never let you be pushed past your limit; he'll always be there to help you come through it." (I Corinthians 10:13, MSG)

7. _____ another believer.
"Brethren, if a man is overtaken in any trespass, you who are spiritual _____ such a one in a spirit of gentleness, considering yourself lest you also be tempted." (Galatians 6:1, NKJV)

"Live creatively, friends. If someone falls into sin, forgivingly re-store him, saving your critical comments for yourself. You might be needing forgiveness before the day's out. Stoop down and reach out to those who are oppressed. Share their burdens, and so complete Christ's law. If you think you are too good for that, you are badly deceived." (Galatians 6:1-3, MSG)

8.   Jesus was tempted and did _____ _____.
"For we do not have a High Priest who cannot sympathize with our weaknesses, but was in all points tempted as we are, yet _____ _____." (Hebrews 4:15, NKJV)

"Now that we know what we have—Jesus, this great High Priest with ready access to God—let's not let it slip through our fingers. We don't have a priest who is out of touch with our reality. He's been through weakness and testing, experienced it all—all but the sin. So let's walk right up to him and get what he is so ready to give. Take the mercy, accept the help." (Hebrews 4:14-16, MSG)

9.   _____ yourself to _____.
"Therefore _____ to _____. Resist the devil and he will flee from you." (James 4:7, NKJV)

"So let God work his will in you. Yell a loud no to the Devil and watch him scamper. Say a quiet yes to God and he'll be there in no time. Quit dabbling in sin. Purify your inner life. Quit playing the field. Hit bottom, and cry your eyes out. The fun and games are over. Get serious, really serious. Get down on your knees before the Master; it's the only way you'll get on your feet." (James 4:7-10, MSG)

10. Don't give the _____ any opportunities in your life.

"… nor give place to the _____." (Ephesians 4:27, NKJV)

"Go ahead and be angry. You do well to be angry—but don't use your anger as fuel for revenge. And don't stay angry. Don't go to bed angry. Don't give the Devil that kind of foothold in your life." (Ephesians 4:26-27, MSG)

11. _____ has already worked it out for you.
"And we know that _____ causes everything to work together for the good of those who love God and are called according to his purpose for them." (Romans 8:28, NLT)

"What shall we say about such wonderful things as these? If God is for us, who can ever be against us?" (Romans 8:31, NLT)

"Can anything ever separate us from Christ's love? Does it mean he no longer loves us if we have trouble or calamity, or are persecuted, or hungry, or destitute, or in danger, or threatened with death?" (Romans 8:35, NLT)

"No, despite all these things, overwhelming victory is ours through Christ, who loved us. And I am convinced that nothing can ever separate us from God's love. Neither death nor life, neither angels nor demons, neither our fears for today nor our worries about tomorrow—not even the powers of hell can separate us from God's love. No power in the sky above or in the earth below—indeed, nothing in all creation will ever be able to separate us from the love of God that is revealed in Christ Jesus our Lord." (Romans 8:37-39, NLT)

12. You have the _____ in _____ _____.
"But thank God! He gives us _____ over sin and death through our Lord _____ _____." (I Corinthians 15:57, NLT)

The power over sin has not been given to you as a believer because you are born-again. The following scriptures let us know that even as a believer in Christ, there will always be a fight between your flesh and your spirit.

13. The _____ is willing but the _____ is _____.
"Watch and pray, lest you enter into temptation. The _____ indeed is willing, but the _____ is _____." (Matthew 26:41, NKJV)

"When he came back to his disciples, he found them sound asleep. He said to Peter, "Can't you stick it out with me a single hour? Stay alert; be in prayer so you don't wander into temptation without even knowing you're in danger. There is a part of you that is eager, ready for anything in God. But there's another part that's as lazy as an old dog sleeping by the fire." (Matthew 26:40-41, MSG)

"But I say, walk habitually in the [Holy] Spirit [seek Him and be responsive to His guidance], and then you will certainly not carry out the desire of the sinful nature [which responds impulsively without regard for God and His precepts]. For the sinful nature has its desire which is opposed to the Spirit, and the [desire of the] Spirit opposes the sinful nature; for these [two, the sinful nature and the Spirit] are in direct opposition to each other [continually in conflict], so that you [as believers] do not [always] do whatever [good things] you want to do." (Galatians 5:16-17, AMP)

The New Living Translation says...

"So I say, let the Holy Spirit guide your lives. Then you won't be doing what your sinful nature craves." (Galatians 5:16, NLT)

Paul refers to the Corinthian's as carnal-minded people:

"And I, brethren, could not speak to you as to spiritual people but as to carnal, as to babes in Christ. I fed you with milk and not with solid food; for until now you were not able to receive it, and even now you are still not able; for you are still carnal. For where there are envy, strife, and divisions among you, are you not carnal and behaving like mere men?" (I Corinthians 3:1-3, NKJV)

They were still acting spiritually immature, but had professed salvation, yet in many ways are still living according to their old fleshly nature. The truth is only God knows for sure if a carnal-minded believer is born-again or not. A carnal-minded believer is an individual not growing spiritually not because they don't have the Holy Spirit, but because they are not growing in grace and in the knowledge of Christ. The carnal-minded believer tries to use carnal methods to obtain spiritual goals. The Greek word for carnal is *sarkikos*, which means fleshly. In Latin and French, the word *carna* means sensual. The word carnival comes from two words *carne* and *vale*, which means "farewell flesh". The word carnival was something that they had before the season of Lent. During Lent, they will practice farewell to the flesh and enjoy pleasures to the flesh, so just before Lent, they would gorge food and get drunk to satisfy the flesh in every possible way. Then, they would be able to do without such things during Lent. A good example of this will

94

be at the Mardi Gras's, which means *Fat Tuesday* and refers to the Tuesday before Lent begins. Paul describes this in Philippians chapter three verse nineteen.

"… whose end is destruction, whose god is their belly, and whose glory is in their shame— who set their mind on earthly things." (Philippians 3:19, NKJV)

"Stick with me, friends. Keep track of those you see running this same course, headed for this same goal. There are many out there taking other paths, choosing other goals, and trying to get you to go along with them. I've warned you of them many times; sadly, I'm having to do it again. All they want is easy street. They hate Christ's Cross. But easy street is a dead-end street. Those who live there make their bellies their gods; belches are their praise; all they can think of is their appetites." (Philippians 3:17-19, MSG)

What is a carnal-minded believer and what are the evidences? It's wherever you see strife, division, and envy in your life and it feels like you are at a circus. To other people that are watching you it is very entertaining and funny, but you feel like you are at the carnival either enjoying yourself or you can't wait to leave, because you are tired of the struggles of your flesh. Your life feels like you are on a roller coaster ride up, down, sideways, and upside down. Or perhaps like a merry-go-round your whole world is spinning around, but you're just repeating what you have already started. In other words, you have been there and done that. Paul said that a carnal-minded believer is the baby that started out on baby formula milk and years later, they are still drinking the baby formula milk, but actually by now, they should be on solid foods. First

Corinthian's chapter three verse two says that the carnal-minded believer is an individual who has been born-again, but still lives outside the Kingdom of God system, which is God's ways of doing things.

This believer is like the Corinthian's they are born-again, but still thinking on carnal or fleshly ways of doing things. The carnal believer is not growing, maturing, or developing. There are no accomplishments, except for becoming a believer in Christ. The carnal-minded believer cannot walk, talk, understand, follow instructions, help, serve, fight battles, clean their self, feed their self, or pull their self up out of trouble. They are born-again but mentally, they are still a baby and a baby should not be in a diaper at age four, ten, or twenty. Neither shall a born-again believer in Christ be at the same mentality that they were in when they first gave their life to Jesus. Every one of us was born into carnality with selfishness.

"Behold, I was brought forth in iniquity, And in sin my mother conceived me." (Psalms 51:5, NKJV)

The preceding scripture is one of many scriptures that prove that we were born into sin naturally, but also when we became believers in Christ, the carnal nature remained in you. Read the following scripture:

"… for you are still carnal. For where there are envy, strife, and divisions among you, are you not carnal and behaving like mere men?" (I Corinthians 3:3, NKJV)

Carnality is not removed at conversion, because the fruits of carnality of the Corinthian's after conversion was their strife and divisions. The Bible even gives us a longer list of fruits of carnality:

"Now the doings (practices) of the flesh are clear (obvious): they are immorality, impurity, indecency, Idolatry, sorcery, enmity, strife, jealousy, anger (ill temper), selfishness, divisions (dissensions), party spirit (factions, sects with peculiar opinions, heresies), Envy, drunkenness, carousing, and the like. I warn you beforehand, just as I did previously, that those who do such things shall not inherit the kingdom of God." (Galatians 5:19-21, AMPC)

"It is obvious what kind of life develops out of trying to get your own way all the time: repetitive, loveless, cheap sex; a stinking accumulation of mental and emotional garbage; frenzied and joyless grabs for happiness; trinket gods; magic-show religion; paranoid loneliness; cutthroat competition; all-consuming-yet-never-satisfied wants; a brutal temper; an impotence to love or be loved; divided homes and divided lives; small-minded and lopsided pursuits; the vicious habit of depersonalizing everyone into a rival; uncontrolled and uncontrollable addictions; ugly parodies of community. I could go on. This isn't the first time I have warned you, you know. If you use your freedom this way, you will not inherit God's kingdom." (Galatians 5:19-21, MSG)

According to the Word of God, anyone that practices the seventeen works of the flesh shall not inherit the Kingdom of God, unless they confess their fleshly carnal desires.

14. To be _____ minded is _____ but to be _____ minded is _____ and _____.

"For to be _____ minded is _____, but to be _____ minded is life and _____. Because the _____ mind is enmity against God; for it is not subject to the law of God, nor indeed can be. So then, those who are in the flesh cannot please God." (Romans 8:6-8, NKJV)

"Those who think they can do it on their own end up obsessed with measuring their own moral muscle but never get around to exercising it in real life. Those who trust God's action in them find that God's Spirit is in them—living and breathing God! Obsession with self in these matters is a dead end; attention to God leads us out into the open, into a spacious, free life. Focusing on the self is the opposite of focusing on God. Anyone completely absorbed in self ignores God, ends up thinking more about self than God. That person ignores who God is and what he is doing. And God isn't pleased at being ignored." (Romans 8:5-8, MSG)

To be carnally-minded means that you are separated from fellowship with God. But, one thing is for sure when you are living in the flesh and you are a born-again believer in Christ; you do not have any fellowship with God.

"Peter said to Him, "You shall never wash my feet!" Jesus answered him, "If I do not wash you, you have no part with Me." Simon Peter said to Him, "Lord, not my feet only, but also my hands and my head!" Jesus said to him, "He who is bathed needs only to wash his feet, but is completely clean; and you are clean, but not all of you." (John 13:8-10, NKJV)

Jesus is saying that He will not fellowship with anyone who is committing sin or continuing to live in the flesh, so in order for Peter to have fellowship with Jesus, he had to let Jesus wash his feet. A believer that is carnally-minded will not obey the law of God, because they are submitting to sin and when the mind stops rebelling, it will not entertain sin. As long as your mind and heart lives in rebellion, you cannot please God. Whenever you set your affections on things of the flesh, you will fulfill them. Your affections should always be set on things above, not things below.

"Set your mind on things _____, not on things on the _____." (Colossians 3:2, NKJV)

If you set your affections on things of the Spirit, you will not commit sin. Remember that the carnal-minded believers in Corinth received the giver in their life, but their focus became more on the gift, rather than the Giver of the gifts. Anytime you put trust in the fruit more than the Root that is your supplier of the fruit, you will always be headed in the wrong direction for your life.

A carnal believer suffers from "arrested development;" they have not grown as they should have. One thing I want you to realize is that it does not matter how long a person has been a believer in Christ, because it has nothing to do with their level of spiritual maturity. You did not become a believer to stay a baby; you became a believer to grow into the image of Jesus.

Remember that a carnal believer is still on milk spiritually, but as they mature, they are supposed to move beyond the baby milk of the Word into the whole milk and solid food of the Word.

"For though by this time you ought to be teachers, you need someone to teach you again the first principles of the oracles of God; and you have come to need milk and not solid food. For everyone who partakes only of milk is unskilled in the word of righteousness, for he is a babe. But solid food belongs to those who are of full age, that is, those who by reason of use have their senses exercised to discern both good and evil." (Hebrews 5:12-14, NKJV)

"I have a lot more to say about this, but it is hard to get it across to you since you've picked up this bad habit of not listening. By this time you ought to be teachers yourselves, yet here I find you need someone to sit down with you and go over the basics on God again, starting from square one—baby's milk, when you should have been on solid food long ago! Milk is for beginners, inexperienced in God's ways; solid food is for the mature, who have some practice in telling right from wrong." (Hebrews 5:11-14, MSG)

The preceding scripture explains to us the very reason some people are not growing in the Word of God. They do not want to go any deeper into the study of the Word; they are satisfied and content where they're at. If you try to encourage and lead some believers in growing spiritually through the Word of God, they will begin to get "spiritual indigestion". They don't want to grow; they're just satisfied with coming to a church building week after week and putting their mind in neutral and never having to think. In other words, as long as you keep it simple and appeal to their baby needs by telling a few stories, they are happy, but when you begin to challenge them to take them deeper in the Word of God, which will cause spiritual growth in their life, they begin to get an upset stomach. The carnal-minded believer will never crawl out of the nursery until they study and be consistent with their walk in the Word of God.

1. Babies are by nature selfish human beings. They care about no one but themselves. They don't care how tired mom and dad are! They don't care about anything else in the world but themselves! As long as they are the center of attention and their needs are being met, they are fine. But, when something is wrong in their world, they cry, whine, and complain until someone does it their way. The same is true in the life of the carnal believer. The focus is always on themselves. It doesn't matter what's best for the church or other individuals, all that matters is how it affects them personally. When a carnal believer is unhappy, everyone knows it! How? They act like a big baby, calling attention to themselves.

2. Babies want their way and they are prepared to fight for it! They don't care; they will take it by force what they think is theirs. You get a couple of babies together and there will be strife and discord. Remember this anytime there is trouble in your church, home, family, or friends among believers in Christ, there is a baby somewhere still on baby formula and needs to grow up.

NOTES

6

The Spiritual-Minded Believer

"But the spiritual man [the spiritually mature Christian] judges all things [questions, examines and applies what the Holy Spirit reveals], yet is himself judged by no one [the unbeliever cannot judge and understand the believer's spiritual nature]." (I Corinthians 2:15, AMP)

Paul's description of the spiritual man is that he or she has the mind of Christ. To have the mind of Christ does not mean that we have reached a level of perfection equal to Jesus. Having the mind of Christ means that Christ shares with us His spiritual wisdom that enables us to see life from a heavenly perspective; to help us make decisions that are wise for now and eternity. The question that you might be wondering is how does a person become a spiritual man?

First of all, to be a spiritual man, you have to become a born-again believer in Christ by the Holy Spirit.

"For by one [Holy] Spirit we were all baptized into one body, [spiritually transformed—united together] whether Jews or Greeks (Gentiles), slaves or free, and we were all made to drink of one [Holy] Spirit [since the same Holy Spirit fills each life]." (I Corinthians 12:13, AMP)

Secondly, the spiritual man's life is under the control of God's Spirit.

"… but just as it is written [in Scripture], "Things which the eye has not seen and the ear has not heard, And which have not entered the heart of man, All that God has prepared for those who love him [who hold Him in affectionate reverence, who obey Him, and who gratefully recognize the benefits that He has bestowed]." For God has unveiled them and revealed them to us through the [Holy] Spirit; for the Spirit searches all things [diligently], even [sounding and measuring] the [profound] depths of God [the divine counsels and things far beyond human understanding]. For what person knows the thoughts and motives of a man except the man's spirit within him? So also no one knows the thoughts of God except the Spirit of God. Now we have received, not the spirit of the world, but the [Holy] Spirit who is from God, so that we may know and understand the [wonderful] things freely given to us by God." (I Corinthians 2:9-12, AMP)

Through the indwelling presence of the Holy Spirit, God reveals to us His deep spiritual truth. The Holy Spirit's truth includes God's plan of salvation, as well as how to live the Christian life. The spiritual man is also one who lives supernaturally, which means that he lives a spiritual life. You should be living your life not in your old nature, but you should be living your life in the power of the Holy Spirit. Remember, as I stated earlier, every born-again believer in Christ has two natures, which is the

106

Adamic nature and a new spiritual nature. The spiritual man allows Christ to rule his life. Jesus is not just present, He is preeminent. Jesus also does not simply reside in the spiritual man's life; He presides over the spiritual man's life. Let's take another look at our beginning scripture:

"But he who is spiritual judges all things, yet he himself is rightly judged by no one." (I Corinthians 2:15, NKJV)

The word "Judges" means to examine or discern. The spiritual man is alive in the spirit, equipped by the Spirit and is open to the truth of God. The truth of God is not foolish to the spiritual man but it is a fountain of life to him, as good physical food is great for the body spiritual food is good soul food for the spiritual man. The ability to receive and understand the deep things of God does not depend upon your intelligence quotient (I.Q.) or academic ability. Understanding the things of God is accomplished through the ministry of the Holy Spirit in the life of a believer that is yielded to the Word of God.

"But when He, the Spirit of Truth, comes, He will guide you into all the truth [full and complete truth]. For He will not speak on His own initiative, but He will speak whatever He hears [from the Father—the message regarding the Son], and He will disclose to you what is to come [in the future]." (John 16:13, AMP)

"Now when they saw the boldness and unfettered eloquence of Peter and John and perceived that they were unlearned and untrained in the schools [common men with no educational advantages], they marveled; and they recognized that they had been with Jesus." (Acts 4:13, AMPC)

"This is what Elihu, son of Barakel the Buzite, said: "I'm a young man, and you are all old and experienced. That's why I kept quiet and held back from joining the discussion. I kept thinking, 'Experience will tell. The longer you live, the wiser you become.' But I see I was wrong—it's God's Spirit in a person, the breath of the Almighty One, that makes wise human insight possible. The experts have no corner on wisdom; getting old doesn't guarantee good sense. So I've decided to speak up. Listen well! I'm going to tell you exactly what I think." (Job 32:6-10, MSG)

The phrase "yet He himself is rightly judged by no one" means that nonbelievers cannot figure Him out, because a spiritual man's life is a mystery to the natural man. The natural man cannot understand why the spiritual man has peace, joy, and faith in the midst of life's trials. Even though the spiritual man has standards and convictions, he continues to live them out and is not bothered by them. The spiritual man is a constant source of amazement to the carnal and natural man. The bottom line is the spiritual man is a spirit-led man.

Well the natural man has a "human parentage," the spiritual man has a "divine parentage". As a believer, you must realize that all life comes from a pre-existing life. God did not get His start from start; God started start, so then therefore start came out of God. So, regardless to what others may say, there is no such thing as a "Spontaneous Generation" of life. There is not one life that can be born without the planting of living seed. As there is the planting of seed for a human life between a father and a mother in the natural world, there is a father and mother in the spiritual world. The Holy Spirit is the father and the human heart is the womb, or mother, into which the seed of the Word of God is planted. If the seed in the natural world is lifeless and dead, there will never be anything alive that will be birthed and grow, and if the seed of the Word of God is not received and nurtured by the Holy Spirit when it falls into the human heart, there will never be any new life. This explains why a man or a woman can read and study the scriptures in the Word of God, but if they never nurture or conceive the Word which they have read and studied, they will not grow. The purpose of the new birth is to impart a new nature and this nature is spiritual according to the following scripture:

1. "That which is born of the _____ is _____, and that which is born of the _____ is _____." (John 3:6, NKJV)

"There is therefore now no condemnation to those who are in Christ Jesus, who do not walk according to the flesh, but according to the Spirit. For the law of the Spirit of life in Christ Jesus has made me free from the law of sin and death. For what the law could not do in that it was weak through the flesh, God did by sending His own Son in the likeness of sinful flesh, on account of sin: He condemned sin in the flesh, that the righteous requirement of the law might be fulfilled in us who do not walk according to the flesh but according to the Spirit. For those who live according to the flesh set their minds on the things of the flesh, but those who live according to the Spirit, the things of the Spirit. For to be carnally minded is death, but to be spiritually minded is life and peace. Because the carnal mind is enmity against God; for it is not subject to the law of God, nor indeed can be. So then, those who are in the flesh cannot please God. But you are not in the flesh but in the Spirit, if indeed the Spirit of God dwells in you. Now if anyone does not have the Spirit of Christ, he is not His. And if Christ is in you, the body is dead because of sin, but the Spirit is life because of righteousness. But if the Spirit of Him who raised Jesus from the dead dwells in you, He who raised Christ from the dead will also give life to your mortal bodies through His Spirit who dwells in you. Therefore, brethren, we are debtors—not to the flesh, to live according to the flesh. For if you live according to the flesh you will die; but if by the Spirit you put to death the deeds of the body, you will live." (Romans 8:1-13, NKJV)

2. "And this is the testimony: that God has given us eternal life, and this life is in His Son. He who has the Son has _____; he who does not have the Son of God does not have _____." (I John 5:11-12, NKJV)

3. "For you died, and your _____ is hidden with _____ in _____. When Christ who is our life appears, then you also will appear with Him in glory." (Colossians 3:3-4, NKJV)

Now, your life is hidden with Christ in God and your life is not yours to give up once you have already given it up. When you become born again you lost your old life to find your new life and then hid your life within Christ. So now your life is his life and when he appears we will also appear with him and glory.

4. "Therefore, if _____ is in _____, he is a _____ creation; old things have passed away; behold, all things have become new." (II Corinthians 5:17, NKJV)

NOTES

7

The Natural Man

"But the natural [unbelieving] man does not accept the things [the teachings and revelations] of the Spirit of God, for they are foolishness [absurd and illogical] to him; and he is incapable of understanding them, because they are spiritually discerned and appreciated, [and he is unqualified to judge spiritual matters]." (I Corinthians 2:14, AMP)

The natural man is a man who lives according to nature. He is governed by his intellect and by his natural affection. The natural man has never accepted Jesus Christ as Savior. The natural man does not understand spiritual things and spiritual things are foolish to him, because he cannot process them in a rational manner. The Word of God, promises of God, grace of God, and faith in God does not exist in his mind. The natural man's perceptions do not extend beyond his reason, experiences, and feelings. The natural man lives in a world limited by his finite mind, which means that he is bound by the limitations of his mind and his five senses. The natural man cannot enter the Kingdom of God, for flesh and blood does not inherit the Kingdom of God.

"Jesus answered him, "I assure you and most solemnly say to you, unless a person is born again [reborn from above—spiritually transformed, renewed, sanctified], he cannot [ever] see and experience the kingdom of God." (John 3:3, AMP)

1. What does it mean to be born-again?

"Do not be surprised that I have told you, 'You must be born again [____ from _____ spiritually _____, _____, _____]." (John 3:7, AMP)

The natural man is a person who lives naturally. He might be a member of a local church or a good person, but he is still lost. Whenever he is exposed to the things of God, or to spiritual expression, he becomes very uncomfortable and usually responds in a natural way, such as dropping out, moving out, or getting upset. The natural man is spiritually dead in his sins.

"And you He made alive, who were dead in trespasses and sins," (Ephesians 2:1, NKJV)

"It wasn't so long ago that you were mired in that old stagnant life of sin. You let the world, which doesn't know the first thing about living, tell you how to live. You filled your lungs with polluted unbelief, and then exhaled disobedience. We all did it, all of us doing what we felt like doing, when we felt like doing it, all of us in the same boat. It's a wonder God didn't lose his temper and do away with the whole lot of us. Instead, immense in mercy and with an incredible love, he embraced us. He took our sin-dead lives and made us alive in Christ. He did all this on his own, with no help from us! Then he picked us up and set us down in

114

highest heaven in company with Jesus, our Messiah." (Ephesians 2:1-6, MSG)

A man who is physically dead cannot respond to physical stimulus and a person that is spiritually dead cannot respond to any spiritual stimulus. The word stimulus is something that rouses activity or energy in a person. According to the scripture, it says that the natural man is two parts alive, body and soul, but the primary part, the part of him that can know and respond to God is dead.

"Now may the God of peace Himself sanctify you completely; and may your whole spirit, soul, and body be preserved blameless at the coming of our Lord Jesus Christ." (I Thessalonians 5:23, NKJV)

SEVEN FACTS OF THE NATURAL MAN

1. The natural man's understanding is darkened.
"… having their understanding darkened, being alienated from the life of God, because of the ignorance that is in them, because of the blindness of their heart;" (Ephesians 4:18, NKJV)

2. The natural man cannot receive or perceive the things of the Spirit of God.
"But the natural man does not receive the things of the Spirit of God, for they are foolishness to him; nor can he know them, because they are spiritually discerned." (I Corinthians 2:14, NKJV)

3. The natural man is a child of wrath.

115

"... among whom also we all once conducted ourselves in the lusts of our flesh, fulfilling the desires of the flesh and of the mind, and were by nature children of wrath, just as the others." (Ephesians 2:3, NKJV)

4. The natural man is at enmity with God and cannot please God. "Because the carnal mind is enmity against God; for it is not subject to the law of God, nor indeed can be. So then, those who are in the flesh cannot please God." (Romans 8:7-8, NKJV)

5. The natural man's heart is deceitful and desperately wicked. "The heart is deceitful above all things, And desperately wicked; Who can know it?" (Jeremiah 17:9, NKJV)

"For from within, out of the heart of men, proceed evil thoughts, adulteries, fornications, murders, thefts, covetousness, wickedness, deceit, lewdness, an evil eye, blasphemy, pride, foolishness." (Mark 7:21-22, NKJV)

6. The natural man is spiritually dead. "And you He made alive, who were dead in trespasses and sins," (Ephesians 2:1, NKJV)

7. The natural man without supernatural help cannot change his character. "Can the Ethiopian change his skin or the leopard its spots? Then may you also do good who are accustomed to do evil." (Jeremiah 13:23, NKJV)

God is not saying that the natural man cannot be a good person, generous, charitable, honest or truthful but what God is saying is that according to Scripture, the natural man is not righteous, which is to be in right standing with God. The natural man is a person that is under the control of fleshly passions that is in contrast with the spiritual man. The natural man has no sense of spiritual values and enjoys living for the world and its carnal pleasures. As I stated earlier, all spiritual things are foolish to him, because he is spiritually dead.

NOTES

8

Salvation is for Everyone

"For it is impossible for those who were once enlightened, and have tasted the heavenly gift, and have become partakers of the Holy Spirit, and have tasted the good word of God and the powers of the age to come, if they fall away, to renew them again to repentance, since they crucify again for themselves the Son of God, and put Him to an open shame." (Hebrews 6:4-6, NKJV)

If a born-again believer sins, it does not mean that they are not saved. But, if the same individual deliberately turns away from the church, teaching, and doctrines of Jesus, this individual has stepped out of the kingdom of light and back into the kingdom of darkness. The words "falling away" do not mean that an individual is not saved anymore. The potential for an individual not to be saved anymore is not just having a rebellious heart towards God, but are also people that are innocently led astray by false doctrines.

GO|STOP SALVATION

Paul expresses his concerns with the Galatians leaving the truth and following a different doctrine of Gospel.

"I marvel that you are turning away so soon from Him who called you in the grace of Christ, to a different gospel," (Galatians 1:6, NKJV)

Paul even expresses his concern to the same group again saying:

"You have become estranged from Christ, you who attempt to be justified by law; you have fallen from grace; You ran well. Who hindered you from obeying the truth?" (Galatians 5:4, 7, NKJV)

Paul's description of the Galatians was that they were "severed from Christ" and "falling from grace". Paul's first letter to Timothy, he predicts that in the last days some believers will be led into following false doctrine.

"Now the Spirit expressly says that in latter times some will depart from the faith, giving heed to deceiving spirits and doctrines of demons, speaking lies in hypocrisy, having their own conscience seared with a hot iron," (I Timothy 4:1-2, NKJV)

Once again, the words "fallen away" are used, which implies a turning away from faith or the revelation of what was once embraced. In Galatians chapter five verse four and seven and first Timothy chapter four verse two, these believers did not fall into sin morally or ethically, they were simply deceived into believing something that was a distortion of the truth.

120

"Therefore, just as through one man sin entered the world, and death through sin, and thus death spread to all men, because all sinned—" (Romans 5:12, NKJV)

Adam's sin poisoned the human race and because of Adam's sin, every man, woman, and child since Adam has been born a sinner.

"And the gift is not like that which came through the one who sinned. For the judgment which came from one offense resulted in condemnation, but the free gift which came from many offenses resulted in justification. For if by the one man's offense death reigned through the one, much more those who receive abundance of grace and of the gift of righteousness will reign in life through the One, Jesus Christ.) Therefore, as through one man's offense judgment came to all men, resulting in condemnation, even so through one Man's righteous act the free gift came to all men, resulting in justification of life. For as by one man's disobedience many were made sinners, so also by one Man's obedience many will be made righteous." (Romans 5:16-19, NKJV)

The term condemn is a legal term meaning "to declare guilty". We are all guilty of sin (singular) because of sins (plural) resulting from our personal disobedience, which caused Adam and Eve to be separated from God in the beginning. God is able to declare the "guilty" individuals "not guilty". Paul explains this in his second letter to the Corinthians:

"For He made Him who knew no sin to be sin for us, that we might become the righteousness of God in Him." (II Corinthians 5:21, NKJV)

This verse shows that imputation was involved in the process of salvation. God imputed our sins to Christ and Christ's righteousness to you and me. To impute something to someone means to credit them with it. Christ credited you and I with His righteousness, including all its rights and privileges. God could not remain just and ignore sin. There was a penalty to be paid, so He suffered death in our place and in doing so, He paid the penalty we had incurred.

If our sins demanded a death that involved eternal separation from God, how could Jesus pay the penalty for our sins and still sit at the right hand of God? Shouldn't Jesus be separated from God, since He took our place? The answer to the above question is yes. For Jesus Christ to pay for our sins, He would have to suffer the punishment originally intended for you and me.

"Now when the sixth hour had come, there was darkness over the whole land until the ninth hour. And at the ninth hour Jesus cried out with a loud voice, saying, "Eloi, Eloi, lama sabachthani?" which is translated, "My God, My God, why have You forsaken Me?" (Mark 15:33-34, NKJV)

As Jesus Christ hung on the cross, the separation between God and Him was so real that He did not address God as "My Father;"rather, He cried out, "My God, My God". Their fellowship was broken and the intimacy was gone, and Jesus Christ was alone. Jesus, however, was able to reestablish fellowship with His Heavenly Father.

"But Christ came as High Priest of the good things to come, with the greater and more perfect tabernacle not made with hands, that is, not of this creation. Not with the blood of goats and calves, but with His own blood He entered the Most Holy Place once for all, having obtained eternal redemption." (Hebrews 9:11-12, NKJV)

After Jesus paid the penalty for our sin, He was able to go back into the presence of God and restore the fellowship with God, because of His own righteousness. Sin has always been the barrier between man and God, but Christ had no sin; therefore, there was nothing to keep Him from uniting with His Father, even after a brief time of separation. Jesus' sinlessness made Him the only acceptable sacrifice for sin.

"But as many as received Him, to them He gave the right to become children of God, to those who believe in His name:" (John 1:12, NKJV)

"Now when He was in Jerusalem at the Passover, during the feast, many believed in His name when they saw the signs which He did." (John 2:23, NKJV)

"And this is the will of Him who sent Me, that everyone who sees the Son and believes in Him may have everlasting life; and I will raise him up at the last day." (John 6:40, NKJV)

Can Jesus find you "guilty" after He has already declared you "not guilty"? Which one of your sins did Jesus take to the cross over two-thousand years ago? All of our sins were forgiven at the very moment Jesus died on the cross and we were declared "not guilty". The next time Jesus appears on the earth, His purpose is not to die for our sins that He missed the first time.

123

"For Christ has not entered the holy places made with hands, which are copies of the true, but into heaven itself, now to appear in the presence of God for us; not that He should offer Himself often, as the high priest enters the Most Holy Place every year with blood of another—He then would have had to suffer often since the foundation of the world; but now, once at the end of the ages, He has appeared to put away sin by the sacrifice of Himself. And as it is appointed for men to die once, but after this the judgment, so Christ was offered once to bear the sins of many. To those who eagerly wait for Him He will appear a second time, apart from sin, for salvation." (Hebrews 9:24-28, NKJV)

"Not with the blood of goats and calves, but with His own blood He entered the Most Holy Place once for all, having obtained eternal redemption." (Hebrews 9:12, NKJV)

When Jesus died on the cross, He died for your past sins, present sins, and future sins.

As a born-again believer in Jesus Christ, you are not just acquitted of a crime of sins; you are also forgiven of your sins. To be acquitted of a crime means to be released from all obligations concerning any debts or liabilities. An acquittal is included in forgiveness, but it goes even further. To forgive someone is to except the individual back into fellowship. Forgiveness is also connected to restoration of a fellowship. Whenever an unbeliever puts their trust in Jesus, they are not just acquitted of their sins; they are forgiven.

YOU CAN BE ADOPTED

Apostle Paul used the word adoption in the book of Romans to describe the process by which God establishes a relationship with a man or a woman who trusts Jesus Christ as their Savior.

"For you did not receive the spirit of bondage again to fear, but you received the Spirit of adoption by whom we cry out, "Abba, Father." The Spirit Himself bears witness with our spirit that we are children of God," (Romans 8:15-16, NKJV)

Apostle Paul used the word adoption again in the book of Galatians:

"But when the fullness of the time had come, God sent forth His Son, born of a woman, born under the law, to redeem those who were under the law, that we might receive the adoption as sons." (Galatians 4:4-5, NKJV)

When an unbeliever is declared not guilty through the process of imputation, it's a step in the direction of salvation. It is a relationship made available through adoption.

"Most assuredly, I say to you, he who hears My word and believes in Him who sent Me has everlasting life, and shall not come into judgment, but has passed from death into life." (John 5:24, NKJV)

When an unbeliever becomes a believer, they will never be judged for their sins, because when an unbeliever accepts Jesus in their life, God knows the sins they were still going to commit.

"Blessed be the God and Father of our Lord Jesus Christ, who has blessed us with every spiritual blessing in the heavenly places in Christ, just as He chose us in Him before the foundation of the world, that we should be holy and without blame before Him in love, having predestined us to adoption as sons by Jesus Christ to Himself, according to the good pleasure of His will," (Ephesians 1:3-5, NKJV)

God chose to adopt you as His child before the foundation of the world. Throughout the years, I have heard of a lot of unwanted pregnancies that have led to abortions, but I have also personally been in a courtroom and have adopted children. God has adopted a believer for the same reason. God is more concerned with righteousness than unrighteousness.

"And the Pharisees and scribes complained, saying, "This Man receives sinners and eats with them." So He spoke this parable to them, saying: "What man of you, having a hundred sheep, if he loses one of them, does not leave the ninety-nine in the wilderness, and go after the one which is lost until he finds it? And when he has found it, he lays it on his shoulders, rejoicing. And when he comes home, he calls together his friends and neighbors, saying to them, 'Rejoice with me, for I have found my sheep which was lost!' I say to you that likewise there will be more joy in heaven over one sinner who repents than over ninety-nine just persons who need no repentance." (Luke 15:2-7, NKJV)

The following are two examples that show that God is always concerned about what is lost and not what is found:

THE WOMAN WHO LOST A VALUABLE COIN

"Or what woman, having ten silver coins, if she loses one coin, does not light a lamp, sweep the house, and search carefully until she finds it? And when she has found it, she calls her friends and neighbors together, saying, 'Rejoice with me, for I have found the piece which I lost!' Likewise, I say to you, there is joy in the presence of the angels of God over one sinner who repents." (Luke 15:8-10, NKJV)

THE LOST SON

"Then He said: "A certain man had two sons. And the younger of them said to his father, 'Father, give me the portion of goods that falls to me. ' So he divided to them his livelihood." (Luke 15:11-12, NKJV)

YOU ARE SEALED

As believers, we are sealed in Christ and the primary benefit of being sealed is for protection.

"In Him you also trusted, after you heard the word of truth, the gospel of your salvation; in whom also, having believed, you were sealed with the Holy Spirit of promise, who is the guarantee of our inheritance until the redemption of the purchased possession, to the praise of His glory." (Ephesians 1:13-14, NKJV)

During the tribulation, God will place a seal on 144,000 Jews. The seal will be a visible mark on their forehead.

"And I heard the number of those who were sealed. One hundred and forty-four thousand of all the tribes of the children of Israel were sealed: of the tribe of Judah twelve thousand were sealed; of the tribe of Reuben twelve thousand were sealed; of the tribe of Gad twelve thousand were sealed; of the tribe of Asher twelve thousand were sealed; of the tribe of Naphtali twelve thousand were sealed; of the tribe of Manasseh twelve thousand were sealed; of the tribe of Simeon twelve thousand were sealed; of the tribe of Levi twelve thousand were sealed; of the tribe of Issachar twelve thousand were sealed; of the tribe of Zebulun twelve thousand were sealed; of the tribe of Joseph twelve thousand were sealed; of the tribe of Benjamin twelve thousand were sealed." (Revelation 7:4-8, NKJV)

This mark on the forehead will provide supernatural protection from anything that is happening around them. At the end of the tribulation, this entire group will reappear together to welcome to King.

"Then I looked, and behold, a Lamb standing on Mount Zion, and with Him one hundred and forty-four thousand, having His Father's name written on their foreheads. And I heard a voice from heaven, like the voice of many waters, and like the voice of loud thunder. And I heard the sound of harpists playing their harps. They sang as it were a new song before the throne, before the four living creatures, and the elders; and no one could learn that song except the hundred and forty-four thousand who were redeemed from the earth. These are the ones who were not defiled with women, for they are virgins. These are the ones who follow the Lamb wherever He goes. These were redeemed from among men, being firstfruits to God and to the Lamb. And in their mouth was found no deceit, for they are without fault before the throne of God." (Revelation 14:1-5, NKJV)

The 144,000 Jews mentioned in Revelation had a visible seal place on their forehead. However, as believers in Jesus Christ, our seal is spiritual, not physical.

"Now He who establishes us with you in Christ and has anointed us is God, who also has sealed us and given us the Spirit in our hearts as a guarantee." (II Corinthians 1:21-22, NKJV)

Even though the seal that God will use for the Jews, which is a mark on the forehead will be different than what He would use for believers. As believers in Jesus Christ, our seal is the Holy Spirit which is different, but the meaning and purpose is and will be the same, which is for protection. Just as the physical seal will protect them from losing their physical life, the believer's spiritual seal shows us the longevity of a spiritual life.

As a believer, you are sealed through the "day of redemption," which is the day when the believer's salvation will be complete in the body and spirit.

"And do not grieve the Holy Spirit of God, by whom you were sealed for the day of redemption." (Ephesians 4:30, NKJV)

"Not only that, but we also who have the firstfruits of the Spirit, even we ourselves groan within ourselves, eagerly waiting for the adoption, the redemption of our body." (Romans 8:23, NKJV)

The believer's salvation will not be complete until we receive our new body.

"For this corruptible must put on incorruption, and this mortal must put on immortality." (I Corinthians 15:53, NKJV)

The believer's salvation will not be complete until the end of time, but until then, we are protected by the power of God.

"… who are kept by the power of God through faith for salvation ready to be revealed in the last time." (I Peter 1:5, NKJV)

Since God put the seal in place, He is the only one who can remove or break it. He has decided to keep this seal in place until the believer's salvation is complete.

"And I saw in the right hand of Him who sat on the throne a scroll written inside and on the back, sealed with seven seals. Then I saw a strong angel proclaiming with a loud voice, "Who is worthy to open the scroll and to loose its seals?" And no one in heaven or on the earth or under the earth was able to open the scroll, or to look at it. So I wept much, because no one was found worthy to open and read the scroll, or to look at it." (Revelation 5:1-3, NKJV)

Are you going to perish?

"Do you not know that the unrighteous will not inherit the kingdom of God? Do not be deceived. Neither fornicators, nor idolaters, nor adulterers, nor homosexuals, nor sodomites, nor thieves, nor covetous, nor drunkards, nor revilers, nor extortioners will inherit the kingdom of God. And such were some of you. But you were washed, but you were sanctified, but you were justified in the name of the Lord Jesus and by the Spirit of our God." (I Corinthians 6:9-11, NKJV)

An unbeliever guilty of sexual and unethical summons can find forgiveness through Jesus Christ. Even Paul himself, who was the author of first Corinthian's, was guilty of persecuting the church and taking Christians to prison. Jesus even showed forgiveness to the individuals who were crucifying Him.

"Then Jesus said, "Father, forgive them, for they do not know what they do." And they divided His garments and cast lots." (Luke 23:34, NKJV)

The key ingredient that will keep an unbeliever from perishing is believing in Jesus Christ.

"For God so loved the world that He gave His only begotten Son, that whoever believes in Him should not perish but have everlasting life. For God did not send His Son into the world to condemn the world, but that the world through Him might be saved. "He who believes in Him is not condemned; but he who does not believe is condemned already, because he has not believed in the name of the only begotten Son of God." (John 3:16-18, NKJV)

An unbeliever is judged, because they have not believed in the Son of God. The judgment that God is referring to is not the "judgment seat of Christ," because Paul said that we would appear there for judgment. This cannot take place until after death.

"For we must all appear before the judgment seat of Christ, that each one may receive the things done in the body, according to what he has done, whether good or bad." (II Corinthians 5:10, NKJV)

God cannot be referring to the "great white throne judgment," because this judgment is reserved for men and women after life when the earth has ended. Also, the "great white throne judgment" is described in revelation as a onetime event.

"Then I saw a great white throne and Him who sat on it, from whose face the earth and the heaven fled away. And there was found no place for them. And I saw the dead, small and great, standing before God, and books were opened. And another book was opened, which is the Book of Life. And the dead were judged according to their works, by the things which were written in the books. The sea gave up the dead who were in it, and Death and Hades delivered up the dead who were in them. And they were judged, each one according to his works. Then Death and Hades were cast into the lake of fire. This is the second death. And anyone not found written in the Book of Life was cast into the lake of fire." (Revelation 20:11-15, NKJV)

"For God did not send His Son into the world to condemn the world, but that the world through Him might be saved." (John 3:17, NKJV)

It is not lying, cheating, stealing, gossiping, fornication, or adultery that will send you to hell. It is rejecting Christ and refusing to put your trust in Him for the forgiveness of sin. God loves you! Faith is the key ingredient in gaining salvation, but faith is not the reason why God wants you to be saved. The key ingredient is LOVE!

132

"But God, who is rich in mercy, because of His great love with which He loved us, even when we were dead in trespasses, made us alive together with Christ (by grace you have been saved), and raised us up together, and made us sit together in the heavenly places in Christ Jesus, that in the ages to come He might show the exceeding riches of His grace in His kindness toward us in Christ Jesus. For by grace you have been saved through faith, and that not of yourselves; it is the gift of God, not of works, lest anyone should boast." (Ephesians 2:4-9, NKJV)

The beginning of verse four says... "His great love which He loved us..." The words "through faith" in verse two is very important in this. First of all, the word "through" is translated from the Greek word *dia* which means *an agent*. So, faith was the agent by which God was able to apply His grace to the life of an unbeliever.

NOTES

_____
_____
_____
_____
_____
_____
_____
_____
_____
_____

About the Author

Ray Hampton was born in Oahu, Hawaii, on October 8, 1964. He and his wife, Julia, have extended their hands to many individuals and families who were destitute of daily needs. As a child and teenager, he was raised in Lynnwood, Washington, where he attended elementary, junior high, and high school.

In July 1991, at the age of twenty-six, he realized he had a passion to help people in a great way, so he went out on the street corner of Colby and Hewitt in Everett, Washington, to start feeding the homeless and hungry. At that very moment, his outreach ministry was started with a folding card table, a ten-gallon McDonald's juice container, ten loaves of bread, and ten packages of bologna. He has been doing community outreach consistently for more than twenty-eight years and currently is an author, Church Growth Consultant, entrepreneur, television personality, and public figure. He is known throughout the United States for teaching people how to engage, be equipped, and empowered for evangelism and outreach. He has served as chaplain in a wide range of venues, from the Snohomish County corrections facility to semiprofessional soccer teams, and as a mentor to many National Football League players from the Seattle Seahawks.

He also believes in higher education, having started out at Washington State University and continued his education at A. L. Hardy Academy of Theology. To his acclaim, he currently holds a master's degree in marriage and biblical family counseling and two doctoral degrees, one in ministry and the other in theology. He also served as senior pastor for the Seattle International Church for fifteen years.

Ray Hampton has inspired thousands of homeless, helpless, and hopeless individuals and families for more than twenty-eight years by giving them not only a handout, but also a hand up through his many massive outreach giveaways. These include brand-new toys at the annual "Christmas in the City" toy giveaway and to date more than 90,000 toys have been given to children. In addition, 178,000 meals have been prepared to feed the hungry, thousands of items of clothing, shoes, and over 15,000 backpacks filled with school supplies have been distributed. These are just a few of the major outreaches that have had an impact in people's life.

Ray currently lives in Fort Lauderdale, Florida, with his wife, Julia whom he married at seventeen years old. They have been married for thirty-seven years and have been blessed with seven children and have provided a home to multiple children as foster parents for over twenty-three years. His calling in life is very simple: *find a need and fill it or a hurting heart and heal it*. He continues to provide answers to problems by serving with his palms down and not his palms up.

Made in the USA
Columbia, SC
20 March 2023

13819154R00078